# Ives and Copland

*Parallel Lives Series, No. 1*

# Ives and Copland

## A Listener's Guide

Daniel Felsenfeld

AMADEUS
PRESS

Pompton Plains, NJ • Cambridge, UK

Published in 2004 by

Amadeus Press, LLC
512 Newark Pompton Turnpike
Pompton Plains, New Jersey 07444, USA

Amadeus Press
2 Station Road
Swavesey, Cambridge CB4 5QJ, UK


For sales, please contact

NORTH AMERICA

AMADEUS PRESS, LLC
c/o Hal Leonard Corp.
7777 West Bluemound Road
Milwaukee, Wisconsin 53213, USA
Tel. 800-637-2852
Fax 414-774-3259

UNITED KINGDOM AND EUROPE

AMADEUS PRESS
2 Station Road
Swavesey, Cambridge CB4 5QJ, UK
Tel. 01954-232959
Fax 01954-206040

E-mail: orders@amadeuspress.com
Website: www.amadeuspress.com

Printed in Canada

Library of Congress Cataloging-in-Publication Data

Felsenfeld, Daniel.
Ives and Copland : a listener's guide / by Daniel Felsenfeld.
    p. cm. — (Parallel lives series ; no. 1)
    Includes bibliographical references (p.   ).
    ISBN 1-57467-098-0
        1. Ives, Charles, 1874–1954—Criticism and interpretation. 2. Copland, Aaron,
1900–1990—Criticism and interpretation. I. Title. II. Series.

    ML390.F35 2004
    780'.92'273—dc22

                                                    2004018848

For Robert Levine

# Contents

## Part 2: Listening to the Music

## Part 3: Aspects of Copland and Ives                        117

# Acknowledgments

Despite the presence of a single name on the spine of this book, it is of course never a single person doing any of the work—books, I've come to find out, are written by committee. So thank you all who had the misfortune to hear me whining and fretting about the making of this book, a list too vast to outline here.

God bless the MacDowell Colony, always the most hospitable place on the planet—a cross between a monastery and a five-star hotel—and it was a particular treat to write about Copland in a place he loved deeply, a place so steeped in his own history. To listen to *Appalachian Spring* is always a great experience; to listen to it in the exact place he wrote it, that's touching history. I was not there to write this book, at least as far as they knew (I was composing an opera), so this book is the secret, loving product of my spare time. Special thanks to Michelle, Blake, and Christina for making it extra special. On a whim, I daringly read from the opening to all of the great writers present there, and got amazing questions or comments from Lisa Carey, Michael Chabon, T. Louise Freeman, Erin Flanagan, Carol Irving, John Bisbee, and Katherine Min, so thanks to all of you.

Thanks to Helane Anderson at Boosey and Hawkes, Jennifer Stephens at Sony, and Rebecca Davis at Naxos for helping with scores and recordings, aiding and abetting my study of these works. And to the American Music Center, especially Frank Oteri, for making a place where music from my native land is taken seriously—Charles would have been proud; Aaron was.

Thank you to Lee Hyla, who taught me to listen, taught me that listening is as creative as composing. And to Rachel Cohen, who taught me how to think carefully, and showed me, through her book and her conversations, how small moments matter greatly. I don't pretend to write like her, but hope someday to be able to try.

To the biographers Jan Swafford, Howard Pollock, and Vivian Perlis, and to the conductor Michael Tilson Thomas (none of whom I know personally), thank you for your tireless work and palpable love of both Copland and Ives—this book stands on the shoulders of giants.

Thanks to Ernest Hilbert, my artistic soul mate, for making sure I kept going.

Thanks to the New York set—Stephanie Wright, Marie Mascari, Mark Adamo, John Corigliano, Stacy Frierson, Rick Carrick, Paola Prestini, and especially Elizabeth Gold—who made my being insufferable sufferable, and who reminded me I could do it when I really had epic doubts. How could one do better than all of you?

Thanks to John Cerullo at Amadeus Press for publishing this book, which I hope will help people learn.

But the biggest thanks of all is for Robert Levine, heaven's editor, to whom this book is dedicated, for helping me along, teaching me how to write about music clearly and with integrity (any missteps or clunky sentences are mine, not his), for having the courage to shepherd me into the labyrinthine world of New York's music writers years ago, and for not giving up on me despite my occasional boneheaded blunder, sloppy copy, or slightly overshot deadline.

Messieurs Copland and Ives, it was really great to get to know you.

# Ives and Copland

# Introduction

*American mavericks*—this phrase is closely associated with both Aaron Copland and Charles Ives, considered to be the two composers who built the "American sound" in classical music. Before them, America had composers, to be sure, but either they were all beholden, at least by training, to a Teutonic ideal, studying in Germany and bringing the enlightenment of the Continent to the so-called "New World," or they were imported: Dvořák was brought from Bohemia by well-meaning American patrons to tell us all how to compose, and appointed the task of forging a new kind of music—an American music—out of the attractively primitive melodies of slaves and Indians.

In the great cosmopolitan centers of Boston and New York, classical music was strictly European, with opulent opera companies like the Metropolitan, and orchestras like the Boston Symphony Orchestra and the New York Philharmonic, serving as cultural window dressing, displaying the *zeitgeist* of achieved sophistication. In short, they were designed to project just how much like their European forebears these otherwise provincial American cities had become: classical music was an aperitif, *haute couture* and an evening's entertainment rolled into one; it had little to do with the New World.

To be an American and be a composer was contra the expectations of the major musical institutions, unless one cowed to the far-off Continent where all things Western had their alleged origins. Then along came the steely Charles Ives and the plain-talking Aaron Copland, two artists who could not be more different in spirit or intent, yet whose separate singular aesthetics would not only come to define the quintessential American sound in music—sadly, the sound now aped in Civil War epics and beef commercials—but also the way a composer needed (and still needs) to behave: Copland, the man of the people; Ives, the cantankerous outsider. Copland, the cosmopolitan homosexual who sought to do for Brooklyn what Mozart did for Vienna, the most visible and proactive composer of his day; Ives, the self-reliant Emersonian man, who wrote only for himself, honing his private musical and philosophical aesthetic, making his living selling insurance. Copland of the asphalt jungle; Ives of the woods and the pond. Ives as literate New Englander, facing his own fears in isolation; Copland as the epitome of the American mythos of Horatio Alger's dream-the-impossible-dream spirit, not even brought down by the ruinous machinations of the House of Un-American Activities Committee. Copland playing the rube while being genuinely acculturated; Ives, the technically rough outsider, whose rough-shod exterior masked a deep spirituality.

Even today, an American composer is viewed as either an inside player or an outsider, all through the lens of what Ives and Copland built. To separate the life of a composer from his music misses the point. Copland's Jewishness and homosexuality, his populism and generosity, are as crucial to understanding his output as Ives's grim determinism, macho self-assurance, his hatred of "sissies," and his cathecting the transcendentalists. These things matter; they helped shape these men, who in turn helped define the future of music.

Biographies of composers have particular agendas—often they show a similar arc: the humble beginnings that give gradual way to stardom in the face of critical ambiguity or vituperation, eventually ending in tributes, a coterie, and a humble we-never-knew-ye sort of death. They do little to enlighten the reader about the music, treating the work as a product of the life rather than the other way around. Conversely, a strict analysis, usually on a deep, academic level, generally avoids humanizing a composer; instead it can certainly serve as a guide to the music, but often misses the contextual point. Composers are people, but people who write music. We enjoy hearing about their lives only because we love their work—take away the output, and what are they? But in order to better understand their work on a deeper level, we need to understand the facts of their upbringing, the context in which they created, even if the portraits are not always complimentary or the stories inherently compelling. To view composers atop a Parnassus does them a disservice equal to reducing them to their basest, least interesting musical output.

It is not always the most famous works that serve to best explain. While, yes, one should address Copland's *Appalachian Spring* and *Fanfare for the Common Man,* much is to be gained from his masterpiece, the *Piano Variations.* Ives is perhaps best known for his *Three Places in New England* or *The Unanswered Question,* but his deepest and most profound work is the song *General William Booth Enters into Heaven,* a piece not often performed or recorded, but essential to those desiring a way into the thorny spirit of this great composer.

This author's sincerest hope is that you come to love the work of these composers in a new way if you are already an initiate, and in the "right" way if this is all new to you. One of the contemporary misconceptions about so-called "classical" music is that it is beauty that simply washes over you, transcendent and resplendent in itself, and the listener either cottons to it or not. A book such as this can make, without much effort, for careful, thoughtful listening—the ability not just to enjoy the work for its outermost layer, but to hear in it what the composer probably hoped you would. No technical jargon, no charts or graphs, no elementary score reading needed, just open ears and a passion not just for listening but for understanding, and thereby loving, the work of these two truly original, truly brilliant artists.

# How to Listen

In the latter part of the twentieth century, a lot of the touted and so-called "great" modern music sent audiences running back to the classics, to earlier, less terrifying times when music sought to uplift, entertain, and move. Divisive arguments and a bunker mentality among composers became part and parcel for participation, and bitter feuds were waged, an enthusiastic and responsive audience numbering among the casualties. Strains of thought became fractured, and the first aims of the individual aesthetic camps grew more and more occluded, so much so that the not-yet-begun sifting process of the recently closed musical century might well prove an impossible task; these schisms were just not that simple.

One of the main animals to be born of this tumult was the "educated audience," the perfect collective of listeners drummed up *ex nihilo* by some powerful composers who sought surface complexity (as opposed to emotional complexity) as the highest possible musical end, likening their compositions to top-level science or mathematics, much as Wittgenstein tried to do with his vivisection of language and the Frankfurt school with thought: tough to understand was the order of the day; these composers wrote music for their all-but-imaginary ideal audience—in short, they wrote for themselves, for each other, and for the future generations of upper-echelon *Ubermenschen* that never came.

An audience at a concert would have to be, they believed, the equal of those who might attend a conference on physics or a lecture on advanced mathematics: pre-informed, committed, and of a certain intellectual caliber—you had to have done your homework. But let's face it: who holds season tickets to physics lectures? The attitude among some artists was that they need only put forth the theories, design the pieces, and that it was the audience's responsibility to ferret out the coherence, an aesthetic agenda less than popular among music lovers. Some stayed; most fled—it was difficult to find any beauty among a whole phalanx of naked emperors, and the (as always) less-than-enlightened critics, who feared being left behind, leapt on the often mercurial bandwagons, screaming about this or that genius, so-called progressive minds guiding poor souls through the longhair morass, forcing audiences, inevitably, out of the concert hall. After all, nobody likes to be told they are stupid because they found a piece of music to be beautiful.

## What Is There to Get?

So just how much does one have to understand beforehand in order to appreciate the music of Copland or Ives, composers who worked during these difficult times? It is a question with no simple answer, but there are a few basic guidelines; there is some work involved, but fear not, it is not as difficult as you might think. It just requires a little committed interest, and a willingness to listen in a different way.

Listening, like reading or watching a movie, is an active, involved process, and the deeper you want to go, the greater will be your reward. If you simply glance at a painting, or turn on a film in the background while cleaning or having a meal, you will no doubt miss not only the subtleties, but the obvious as well, and thereby get less out of it than if you spend quiet, contemplative time, taking more than a moment to absorb the painting or following closely the cinematic narrative. The same is true of listening to music: the more concentrated time you spend, the more the music—especially good music—will come to mean. Joseph Conrad wrote of there being no such thing as a reader but a re-reader, and the same is true of music: hearing a piece several times inevitably offers a deeper understanding than hearing it only once.

It is not, however, the role of the concert audience to know everything that a composer knows, any more than it is the role of a moviegoer to be as deeply conversant in lenses, cinematography, art direction, and lighting as a filmmaker. Rather, the sort of active listening needed is what is required of a reader of the average mystery novel: to be involved, engaged, wanting to understand, but not necessarily technically fluent. In the same way you might follow the aims and ambitions of the characters or the intentionally confusing and trap-laden plot twists of a Simenon or Agatha Christie novel, you might also follow the edges, flashpoints, and exciting turns of a musical composition. In fact, the most appealing music is often put together—intentionally or not—in much the same fashion as a mystery novel: there are limited characters, an enclosed location, red herrings with which the author sets out to baffle, amuse, befuddle, obfuscate, and throw you off the scent. But ultimately the best works give you the goods, revealing themselves for what they are and drawing things to an appropriate and fulfilling—and often thrilling—close.

It is important to know that there are many different ways to listen effectively (and effective—as opposed to "right"—listening is our aim). Each way is suited to the type of music, the intentions of the composer, the individual listener and his or her level of experience, and even the place where one is actually sitting while listening. It would be unwise to listen to a four-hour Wagner opera at the Vienna Staatsoper in the same

way as one might listen to a three-minute song by Debussy at a
conservatory student's graduate recital; Mozart's serenades are
for a different audience than his symphonies, and the Beethoven
of the late quartets requires a certain kind of attention that the
Beethoven of the piano bagatelles does not. Yes, it is all music,
and ought to be listened to with care, but one hears differently
in a concert hall than one does in one's car or when listening
to one's portable iPod device, and the intelligent listener makes
concessions for all of these factors, cultivating, in the end, his
or her own methods.

## A Listening Calculus

When attempting to think critically about a piece of music (on
whatever level), there are three questions to ask:

1. What do you, the listener, feel the composition itself is
   attempting to do?
2. Does it accomplish it?
3. Was the venture worthwhile?

Each of these questions intentionally becomes progressively
less objective (the latter is where "opinion" ought to be slotted),
and this line of inquiry is (or certainly should be) the fulcrum
of criticism, regardless of the level of the listener's expertise.
After all, to expect the same from an episode of *The Simpsons*
as you might from a novel by Henry James is completely
absurd, because those ventures—as good or bad as you might
find them—have completely different aims. It is ludicrous to
even draw a comparison. The same goes for expecting out of
Copland what you might expect out of Wagner (or the Beatles
or Charles Mingus or the Who—or even Ives).

Even though analysis is a creative venture, with no one "right" way to do it, there are accepted techniques and an involved vocabulary that make for a more thorough, more adept listener—you can go as deep as you like into this, but it is not necessary for understanding. When reading poetry, for example, one can seek the deepest traditional root, understand the instincts of the poet, delve into the technical mechanisms, or one can simply—with a quick introduction—allow oneself the enjoyment one gets from a slightly careful, enthusiastic reading. The same holds true for music. Musicians analyze in order to discover the scaffolding behind the piece, its architecture, its intent, its design; lay listeners need only sort out why the piece works, what makes it cool (or moving or beautiful or sensual or whatever).

With the "Listening" portions of this book, we will examine together the first, most objective, question—understanding what the piece is attempting to accomplish—with regard to specific pieces. The other two questions—Does it accomplish it? and, Was the venture worthwhile?—you the listener will answer with an informed opinion. The aim is neither to persuade you of the music's merits nor to smash idols, but to help you to better answer the three questions outlined above. Listening is a non-stop process: you can never do it too deeply or too well.

# Part 1

## Biographical Sketches

# Aaron Copland

## Young American

"I was born," wrote Aaron Copland in his book *Our New Music*, "on a street in Brooklyn that can only be described as drab. It had none of the garish color of the ghetto, none of the charm of an old New England thoroughfare, nor even the rawness of a pioneer street. It was simply drab. Music was the last thing anyone would have connected with it. In fact, no one had ever connected music with my family or my street. The idea was entirely original with me." And so begins the life of one of the first true-blue American composers.

Copland's parents—Harris Morris Copland and Sarah Mittenthal—were from the Polish and Lithuanian parts of Russia, and both came to New York as Jewish immigrants in the later part of the nineteenth century. Harris owned a successful store in Brooklyn, and was often described by friends as being "all business." Aaron, their fifth child, was born on November 14, 1900, to a family that had never before seen an artist.

Young Aaron showed early interest in the piano, studying for his first years (after he learned what little he could from his mother) with Leopold Wolfsohn, and later went on to more advanced study with Victor Wittgenstein and Clarence Adler. But all the while he indicated a profound and prodigious attraction to composing music, creating songs at age eight, and most of an opera at age eleven. He sought out all the scores he could, particularly those of French composers Ravel and Debussy, and attended concerts at the Brooklyn Academy of Music, where he was particularly knocked sideways by performances of Rimsky-Korsakov's *Scheherazade* and Debussy's *Pelléas and Mélisande* and *L'Après-midi d'un faune.*

As a teenager at Boys' High School, he studied harmony, counterpoint, and form under Rubin Goldmark, gaining a thorough grounding in the High German tradition. He once got whiff of Ives's *Concord Sonata,* but Goldmark feared the influence might improperly influence the obviously talented young Copland, so he was forbidden to look at it. "I immediately asked if I could borrow the music," Copland said (in Vivian Perlis's remarkable and comprehensive oral histories), "but Goldmark said, 'You stay away from it. I don't want you to be contaminated by stuff like that.' I didn't see the piece again until ten years had gone by."

"Before long," wrote Arthur Berger, a composer, critic, and friend who authored the first academic study of the composer, "Copland inevitably found himself disturbed by Goldmark's conservatism. True, Copland, the mature composer, in looking back, now has respect for his first theory teacher's 'excellent grasp of fundamentals' and his ability to 'impart his ideas,' which were all a much needed fillip to a late start." But this experience did not discourage or scare the young composer as much as whet his appetite for the dangerous, or naughty, music that he was forbidden to touch. Boys, after all, will be boys. He would just have to look at the literature that piqued his youthful interest on his own.

Copland read in the magazine *Musical America* about a summer music school for Americans that was going to be opening at the palace of Fontainebleau, not far from Paris. "This was said," said Copland, "to be a gesture of appreciation to America for its friendship during World War I. My parents were less than enthusiastic, but it was known that any well-educated musician had to have the European experience. In the past, that meant Germany, but since the war, the focus of the arts had shifted to France." So Copland packed his things and headed across the Atlantic, his satchel full of scores he had composed, as well as novels in French, his head full of music from his soon-to-be home and his heart full of the desire to become a thoroughly trained, deeply American composer. It was, perhaps, the most important decision of his young life.

# Copland the Cosmopolitan

"It is curiously symbolic," wrote Berger, "that in his eagerness to attend the proposed school at Fontainbleau, he should have been the first to enter his name on the enrollment list. For there he uncovered the potentialities of one of the faculty, Nadia Boulanger, as a teacher for American composers, and he was the first of a long line of creative musicians, among them some of the most accomplished, who came to study with her, encouraged by his glowing accounts of her pedagogy and by his later professional success." From the early twenties until her death in the late seventies, Nadia Boulanger would indeed teach the best and the brightest in American music, including such leading lights as Elliot Carter, Phillip Glass, Leonard Bernstein, Ned Rorem, and a whole host of others. When Copland arrived on her palatial doorstep, she was a young, deeply gifted teacher— not a composer herself, but someone who understood music in a way that filled her protégés with a bit of reverential awe. "I had never before," said Copland, "witnessed such enthusiasm and such clarity in teaching." He had finally found his proper (and much needed) mentor.

"A very long time ago," said Boulanger, nearing the end of her life, "Copland was my student. To let him develop was my great concern. One could tell his talent immediately. The great gift is a demonstration of God. More the student is gifted, more you must be careful not to invade his self. But I hope that I did never disturb him, because then is to no more be a teacher, is to be a tyrant." Copland, already an enthusiast of French music, was thrust into the center of it. Paris in the 1920s was, by all accounts, a spectacular place to be a young artist, the musical scene dominated by a group of composers called *Les Six,* whose musical godfather was the king of quirk, Erik Satie, and whose literary centerpiece was the artistic jack-of-all-trades and *bon vivant* Jean Cocteau. These composers—among them Francis Poulenc, Darius Milhaud, and Arthur Honegger—were creating music for the people, very French (or, as the politics of the day dictated, decidedly *not* German: "Down with Wagner!" was one of their rallying cries), catholic in its plurality, progressive in its harmony, and almost Marxist in that it was written for the people rather than some abstract elite; operas, symphonies, film scores, pop songs, hurdy-gurdy tunes, chamber music, anthems, all commingled, for it was all music to *Les Six,* and the lot of them were extraordinarily prolific.

To leave one's native land, thereby garnering perspective on it, is a fascinating way to come to grips with notions of "home," and Copland, living and working in Paris, was as determined to become American the way that Stravinsky or Mussorgsky were Russian, or Mozart and Brahms were Viennese; he wanted to translate the sounds of his native Brooklyn into notes the way Poulenc and Auric had captured the French café society. Under the equal influence of his teacher Boulanger and the scores of both the then-little-known Viennese composer Gustav Mahler—a recent discovery of his—and the French composer Gabriel Fauré, Copland began to develop his early style, writing orchestral pieces like the uncommissioned ballet *Grohg* (which was about a vampire, written after Copland saw *Nosferatu* in a darkened Paris theater) and a few choral works and songs.

Eventually the composer moved to Paris proper, rooming with Harold Clurman, a distant relative he knew from New York who would later go on to found the very influential Group Theater. They moved to Montparnasse on the Left Bank, a place with dozens of cafés, teeming with artistic life: Gertrude Stein, e. e. cummings, Ezra Pound, Ernest Hemingway,

Sinclair Lewis, Virgil Thomson, Walter Piston, and George Antheil were among the famous Americans living in this small bit of Paris; it was all the intellectual stimulation one could ask for. Copland and Clurman drank plenty together, listened to jazz (which was all the rage), and occasionally were introduced to such luminaries as Proust, Joyce, or Gide, the father figures to this, the "lost" generation.

In the meantime, Copland was doing rather well, winning prizes and establishing himself as the young composer to watch. Returning to the States with Clurman in the late 1920s, he entered a very special New York—one determined to outdo Paris as a cultural center, hot for the newest and sexiest trends. He wrote an Organ Symphony for Nadia Boulanger to perform with the New York Symphony under the baton of her old friend Walter Damrosch, written without ever having heard a note of his own orchestral music played—certainly a brave move for such a young man.

"In those days," wrote Berger, "the public at large regarded a modern composer as something of a naughty boy by whom it was both amused and shocked." Copland, certainly, was no exception, as attests the now apocryphal story of his symphony's first performance: at the end, Damrosch turned to the confused but enthusiastic crowd and said, as legend has it: "If a young man at the age of twenty-three can write a symphony like that, in five years he will be ready to commit murder." Copland was, indeed, back in the land of opportunity.

# Native Son

In those days, jazz captivated the public, and composers were quick to incorporate it into their music, breaking the highbrow/lowbrow barrier. Gershwin's *Rhapsody in Blue* was by-and-large the most influential and successful work along these lines, for a number of reasons: here was this Tin Pan Alley songster, this poor white Jewish boy raised on the wrong side of the tracks, brutally invading Carnegie Hall with his dazzling concerto, which he himself played, perhaps signaling the much-feared revolution. He had sex appeal, power, chops, and, above all, was completely homegrown—no mock-Teutonic music from his pen; his art was thoroughly indigenous. Critics, of course, who liked their high-culture and their "Negro" music to be decisively separate, thought this was an aberration—Copland, in the mind of the public, was not the only one capable of murder, and the poor defenseless citizens of Carnegie Hall needed to be saved from this dark music. In 1925, the same year as *Rhapsody in Blue*, Copland's large-scale orchestral work *Music for the Theater* was greeted with equal critical dissent—his dissonances were too loud, too unresolved, and his harmonies sent the ear spinning. Copland, like Gershwin (and just about any real revolutionary), was widely considered a public charlatan.

His Piano Concerto, a "jazz" work, played in Boston under Koussevitzky with the composer at the keyboard, elicited jeers. "A veritable cabal was formed against this work in 1927," wrote Berger, "among staid Boston listeners, some of whom claimed that such music had no place in Symphony Hall and that Koussevitzky had given it with disguised malice." The conductor wanted, the displeased rabble believed, to show how truly terrible American music could be, and thought Copland was set up as a straw man, an easy target. Regardless of the critical backlash, Copland was invited to play his concerto at the Hollywood Bowl in Los Angeles, after which this divisive, "terrifying" piece was not heard on the concert stage for another sixteen years—and thus the composer decided, perhaps for his career, perhaps in the interest of sanity, or perhaps because he had a penchant for exploration, that this was to be his last "jazz" work. But the revolution was not over.

In the year 1927 musical changes were happening in a very public way. Duke Ellington played at the Cotton Club (usually the province of white people and white people only), and composer George Antheil's *Ballet Mechanique,* considered by some to be the harbinger of the new age, premiered to an astonished Carnegie Hall audience. Copland spent the summer in Europe, to hear *Music for the Theater* and meet the legendary Kurt Weill, who was there watching over the premiere of his opera *Mahagonny.* When Copland returned to the States, it was to take a job at New York City's New School, lecturing on modern music—a job arranged by the unfairly forgotten critic (and early Copland champion) Paul Rosenfeld. Here Copland explained the fundamentals of music to lay audiences, earned a steady paycheck, and had time to compose, though never as much as he would have liked.

But his composing had tapered off a bit—he was reading, lecturing, listening, spending time with his friends, perhaps refilling his well. He did write some smaller works, including two movements for a string quartet that were no more than a trifle to him (Copland never much inclined himself to chamber music, producing throughout his productive life only one major chamber work *per decade),* but likely he was taking a short pause, rethinking his own musical style. Jazz was out. What would be next?

# Modernist, Populist, and All the Steps Between

At the MacDowell Colony, an artists' retreat in New Hampshire—a haven Copland would visit as often as he could—he completed a piano trio called *Vitebsk,* based on a play called *The Dybbuk* he saw in New York. The trio, striking for its ferocity and use of microtones (notes that exist between the keys of the piano, straying from the more conventional "tempered" scale), was the first and only time Copland wrote on decidedly Jewish themes. His soul had been Frenchified, Americanized, and spoke strict Brooklynese in the form of jazz, but he was now getting in touch, through music, with his own Jewishness.

The next two works Copland wrote, the *Symphonic Ode* of 1929 and the *Piano Variations* of 1930, are considered by many Copland admirers (like conductor Michael Tilson Thomas) to be his greatest—the latter his most groundbreakingly "modern" work. The composer was breaking away from his musical roots, both jazz and romantic (read: Brooklyn and a mythic Germany), and defining a new, "modernist" type of sound, one rooted not in key and cadence, but using a single punchy musical cell and saturating the entire piece with that specific sound. This made for pieces, according to the composer, that were ". . . more spare in sonority, more lean in texture." These are the very words, along with descriptives like "stark," that would become easy sound bites to explain Copland's music, for yea- and naysayers alike. Koussevitzky premiered the *Ode* in 1932 in Boston; the

*Variations* were premiered, with the composer at the piano, on a League of Composer's Concert in 1931.

"During these years," Copland wrote, "I began to feel an increasing dissatisfaction with the relations of the music-loving public and the living composer." So he did as he always did, not cursing the proverbial darkness but lighting a candle, organizing concerts and helping to organize a publishing company to look after the music of his day—including the first commercial publication of any songs by Charles Ives. "It seemed to me," said Copland, "that composers were in danger of working in a vacuum." These ventures not only served the music of Copland and Ives, but that of Virgil Thomson, Marc Blitzstein, George Antheil, Henry Cowell, Vladimir Dukelesky (a.k.a. Vernon Duke), and Colin McPhee, among countless others. Copland also, fashioning it presumably after *Les Six*—and no doubt under the sway of his increasingly populist politics—formed a society of like-minded artists called the Young Composer's Group. As always, he wore two inseparable hats: those of the active composer and the proactive organizer of people and events.

During these years, Copland spent a fair amount of time at Yaddo (another colony, this one in Saratoga Springs, New York), not only composing his *Short Symphony* and *Statements for Orchestra*—two works in the same style as the *Piano Variations,* largely forgotten today—but even organizing a concert series there, one that would eventually become the stuff of legends as the Copland-Sessions Concerts. At these concerts, the music of many composers was introduced to the music world, including works by Henry Brant, Ned Rorem, and Charles Ives.

Copland also took a trip to Mexico, to visit his friend, composer Carlos Chavez, someone whom he admired deeply, and who was to conduct a full concert program of the American's work. "I am bringing with me," said Copland, "a young violinist who is pupil, companion, secretary, and friend. His name is Victor Kraft. I'm sure you will like him." With this discreet admission, Copland announced the fact that accompanying him was he who would become his longtime partner and companion. They stayed together in Mexico for several happy months.

As the excitement of the avant 1920s faded into the between-the-wars 1930s, Depression and all, Copland remained characteristically optimistic. His leftist politics—at first, an oddity or counterculture, but certainly not unacceptable; later a definite threat to the existing government—which would eventually get him into a harrowing imbroglio with the House of Un-American Activities Committee, made Copland look to the people, the common man, for inspiration. He even composed a song for the *Worker's Song Book No. 1,* but Copland, naïve to the potential dangers, wrote his anthem ("Into the Streets, May First," composed to be sung at various rallies) with no *nom de plume.*

Copland, in his newest orchestral work, called *El Salón Mexico,* was turning away from his modernist cast and looking to folk tunes or indigenous music—in this case, the boozy, animated sounds found in a Mexican dance hall he wandered into one evening. He had also been commissioned to write a ballet for the Chicago Grand Opera Company, for which he composed the jazz-soaked score *Hear Ye! Hear Ye!* This piece is one mostly forgotten, but it got Copland thinking about ballet again, something that would, in a few short years, become his prime source of inspiration. He also wrote an opera for children, with librettist Edwin Denby, called *The Second Hurricane*—which was presided over by Leonard Bernstein in the pit and young stage director Orson Welles—some children's piano pieces, and an orchestral piece called *Prairie Journal: Music for Radio.*

During this time, he was to cement friendships that would last for the rest of his life. Through his publisher Boosey and Hawkes, Copland was introduced to young composer

Benjamin Britten and his partner (both in concerts and in life) Peter Pears, who would later become neighbors, commissioners, and lifelong friends. The other future friend, and Copland's eventual strongest champion, was a "young Adonis" conductor/composer named Leonard Bernstein, who delivered and performed a recently completed piano reduction of *El Salón México* (an engagement he took while in desperate need of money). Copland, a discreet introvert who seldom spoke of personal matters, surrounded himself with close friends, nonetheless, and these were friendships that would serve for the rest of his days as sources of support, love, inspiration, and even success.

# The Wild West and Hollywood

In 1938, the young Lincoln Kirstein, co-founder of the American Ballet, asked Aaron Copland to write a work for his company. It was presumed the piece would be on an American subject, but when Kirstein broached the idea of using Eugene Loring's scenario about the notorious Billy the Kid, Copland was skeptical: what did a composer from Brooklyn know of this gunslinging criminal from the Wild West? "Lincoln was persuasive," Copland said, "and it did not take him long to convince me that if I could work with Mexican tunes in *El Salón México,* I might try home-grown ones for a ballet." Thus *Billy the Kid* was born, and in spite of a harrowing storm that almost destroyed his manuscript (and the MacDowell colony), the piece was premiered that October, introducing Copland's new style to an enthusiastic public. And Copland, who had spent so many lean years cultivating a prudent, almost stereotypical thrift, began to receive royalty checks.

After his first taste of success, Copland turned to some practical matters: he compiled some music appreciation lectures he had been giving at the New School into his seminal book *What to Listen for in Music,* and he arranged the ballet score of *Billy the Kid* into a free-standing orchestral suite. Around this time he also composed *An Outdoor Overture* (which, though not a staple, is certainly the precursor to *Fanfare for the Common Man)* and the little-known *Lark* for baritone and mixed chorus, presaging his choral masterpiece *In the Beginning.* He also wrote, at the request of his friend Harold Clurman, incidental music for several Group Theater productions, including Irwin Shaw's *Quiet City.* The play itself did not exactly catch on, but

Copland's verdant, ruminative score is a concert staple to this day. He also wrote music for a puppet show at the New York World's Fair and a piece called *John Henry,* commissioned by CBS for a radio program. The legendary bandleader and clarinetist Benny Goodman commissioned Copland to write a concerto, a responsibility he obliged masterfully, drawing on some banked themes from a failed film to compose his Concerto for Clarinet and String Orchestra. But soon the composer got wind of the fact that there was plenty of money to be made writing music for the pictures—as did many of his contemporaries, including no less than Stravinsky, Schoenberg, Prokofiev, and Shostakovich. And so the always itinerant Copland packed his bags and headed west to Hollywood.

His first project was music for a documentary called *The City,* a high-profile, intellectual look at city planning. It was a somewhat successful venture, and based on the work he did, Copland was asked to write music for Lewis Millstone's screen version of Steinbeck's *Of Mice and Men,* an auspicious Hollywood debut to say the least. When writing for the movies, especially during what is now referred to as the "golden age," the composer did not really change his style . . . much. Rather, he tried to find projects to which his music would be well suited. "To some in Hollywood," said Copland, "my music was strange, lean, and dissonant; to others it spoke with a new incisiveness and clarity." He also scored the film of Thornton Wilder's *Our Town.* Wilder was a friend of his from the MacDowell Colony, where, walking up a hill, the two had discussed the possibility of an operatic collaboration, one that never came to be.

From all this film work, Copland was nominated for two Academy Awards and received, in the pages of a magazine called *Modern Music*—then very widely read, now defunct—plenty of excellent critical notices. Not only was he earning money, he was becoming world famous. Due to his work in Hollywood,

concert audiences began to be more interested in his orchestral and chamber music, and doors seemed to be opening up
quickly for the recently-turned-forty composer. But as things
were going well in his own world, skies all over the globe were
darkening with the threat of the coming war. Now was the
time, Copland knew in his generous heart, for all good men to
come to the aid of their country.

# The War Years

"I am impressed," wrote Harold Clurman to Copland, after finding out the composer had been designated a member of the President's Advisory Committee on music. "You are coming into your proper field now: diplomacy." Copland was to be something of a south-of-the-border emissary, a musical ambassador, bringing his knowledge, wide-open mind, and soulful dedication to the "cause" of American music to other parts of the world. Between this and more teaching at Tanglewood— a summer music institute, then solely for American musicians, which he had helped to found—he worked on a piano sonata until his valises, which contained his manuscript sketches, were stolen from the curb outside his home. Much of his material was lost, sadly, but he did manage to finish the piece.

Following the Japanese attack on Pearl Harbor, Copland was commissioned—perhaps not uncoincidentally—to write an orchestral work based on a famous American personage. Originally he set his sights on Walt Whitman, but settled on Abraham Lincoln, writing both text and music to what would become one of his most cherished works, the *Lincoln Portrait*. Immediately following, he composed a fanfare for conductor Eugene Goosens, the so-called *Fanfare for the Common Man,* another of his most remembered works. Then when choreographer Agnes de Mille, still rather unknown, was asked to submit a scenario to the Ballet Russe de Monte Carlo, she expanded an earlier piece in which the dancing evoked horse-back riding (call it "Cowboy chic") and in collaboration with Copland created the epoch-making ballet *Rodeo*. Thus Copland composed three repertoire staples in rapid succession: like most of America, Copland was ablaze with patriotic furor, which translated (thankfully for us) into some of his most slam-bang compositions.

After a brief trip back to Hollywood to write music for the film *North Star,* Copland returned to New York in 1944 to write another ballet, this time for the enigmatic Martha Graham. As he worked, he imagined Graham's singular, frenetic choreographic style and came up with a score he believed would match it, one he called *Music for Martha,* later re-titled *Appalachian Spring,* another gem. Copland, it seemed, had little choice but to write "hits" during this period.

As the war came to an end, a relieved Copland was composing his Third Symphony, to be played under his old friend Koussevitzky. The piece incorporated his now-famous *Fanfare* in a rather rousing way, evoking admonishments from his once-supportive critics, including Paul Rosenfeld. This new Copland, many felt, with his cowboys, Lincoln lauds, and fanfares, had simply sold out. This symphony, his last, was to be the final statement in his more populist mode. Some think the war's ending spelled a dying of personal patriotic zeal for the composer, or that his larger, patriotic works were written not from aesthetic urgency, but rather stemmed from the immediate emergency. Whatever the case, Copland was by no means slowing; just, once again, recasting himself to suit the times.

# From Folk Songs to Tone-Rows

S pinning out of what would be his most successful years, Copland was writing more than ever. After composing the choral work *In the Beginning,* some piano blues pieces, and publishing two books of folk song arrangements, he found himself back in Hollywood in 1948, lured there no doubt by the money, certainly in high demand and able to call the shots after having garnered no less than three Academy Award nominations in as many years. He quickly wrote a score for *The Red Pony,* another Steinbeck adaptation, and *The Heiress,* a film version of Henry James's novel *Washington Square.*

But aside from film scores, Copland had another project in mind. He had always been enthusiastic about the then-little-discussed poet Emily Dickinson, and he set a small selection of her poems (out of well over a thousand) to make his vocal masterpiece *Twelve Poems of Emily Dickinson.* Scored for soprano and piano, it was welcomed by many singers, who lamented a paucity of art songs by the anointed dean of American composers.

In 1950, Copland made a rare dip into chamber music to write a piano quartet, returning once again to his beloved MacDowell Colony to do the bulk of the work. What is most remarkable about this piece, aside from it being a rarity in his output, is that it uses some overtly intellectual discursive techniques, a move then considered a massive *volte-face.* He, like Stravinsky, adopted the recently deceased Arnold Schoenberg's method of composition with twelve tones, a technique where all twelve notes of the chromatic scale take the place of a key. "I felt able," said Copland, "to explore a more abstract and esoteric idiom with chamber music than I could with other types of music." The work puzzled listeners and critics, even staunch Coplandites, because the reigning dogma of the time was an either/or mentality (you were either with Stravinsky *or* Schoenberg, no exceptions, and this was a line that could not easily be toed), and here was Copland, perhaps inadvertently, writing a small but mighty piece, attempting, in his own, recondite, non-glitzy way, to reconcile the two factions.

The one genre Copland had yet to tackle with any seriousness was opera. He had not even attempted one since his youthful *Second Hurricane,* but had, throughout the years, discussed possible collaborations with Thornton Wilder, Arthur Miller, and Clifford Odets, as well as adaptations of well-known American books. Nothing had yet come to bear, but he and his new lover Eric Johns (his relations with Viktor Kraft had drifted years before from discreet amorous pairing to close, lifetime friendship) decided to try their hand. Together, under the terrifying curtain of the cold war, Red scare, and Senator Joseph McCarthy, they wrote *The Tender Land,* a typically American opera about two drifters who corrupt—and permanently change for the worse—a small, innocent town. The music is not the slightest bit blanched by Copland's flirtations with Schoenberg's technique. This is pure, diatonic Copland, in his widest, most roaming-plains Americana mode.

The *Piano Fantasy* of 1957 is Copland's last epic statement, though by no means his last piece. As the always-youthful composer became a "grand old man," certain styles were considered démodé, and many composers who wrote in those styles were forced to either watch their own obsolescence or capitulate, playing the party line. Copland, never one to give in but always curious about the latest things, wrote his most challenging work during the heyday of the new guard, a piece redolent of the bam-smash of the Third Symphony crossed with the modernist introspection and quiet power of the *Piano Variations*. In other words, a summary of his two seemingly diffuse styles, and again, using the piano to break this ground, a safe place to experiment. He used, once again, the *au courant* twelve-tone style, but in a way that is thoroughly his own.

The next few years would see a smattering of compositions, none as potent or important as the works now behind him (but all still as well-wrought and harmonically rich as any). These included: *Dance Panels* (1959), written for choreographer Jerome Robbins; a Nonet for Strings, written on commission from the Dumbarton Oaks Research Library (1960); a final film score, *Something Wild* (1961), which he would subsequently adapt into a suite called *Music for a Great City*; *Connotations* (1962), a twelve-tone orchestral work written for his old friend Leonard Bernstein to conduct at a gala concert to initiate the New York Philharmonic's new performance space (now called Avery Fisher hall); *Emblems*, written for concert band; *Inscape*, a short, pensive orchestral work; a few assorted fanfares, piano pieces (including *Night Thoughts*, an homage to Charles Ives); and his last work, the Duo for Flute and Piano, composed in 1971.

The last seventeen years of Copland's life, he shifted gears, choosing to conduct rather than compose, championing, along with his own music, the work of his established contemporaries. He never took a permanent post, even when one was offered, choosing instead the itinerant touring life. For eleven years, terminating with his last concert in 1982 (when his memory loss was beginning to become an obstacle for the octogenarian), he played all over the world, with groups ranging from the Boston Symphony Orchestra and the New York Philharmonic to student ensembles, opera companies, and youth orchestras. Copland was as generous a conductor as he was a composer.

Copland died on December 2, 1990, a few weeks after his ninetieth birthday, and the service—one Copland, as he knew the end was coming, insisted be "purely musical"—was reported in the *New York Times:* "Not every memorial concert," wrote John Rockwell, "ends with a standing ovation. This one did, not only for the quality of the music making, but also for the continuing affection with which Copland's memory is held by the musical public."

# Charles Ives

## "Don't Pay Too Much Attention to the Sounds, You May Miss the Music"

O n October 20, 1874, Charles Ives was born into a family weaned on the ideas he would come to hold most dear: music, transcendentalism, and the love of the land; they were salt-of-the-earth New England people. His father, George E. Ives, was a prodigiously talented musician himself, and his mother, Mary Elizabeth Pamelee, was a well-known local choral singer. They lived in the affluent town of Danbury, Connecticut, and the home into which young Charles Ives was born—the "old Ives house" it was called—was a tastefully furnished, crowded Victorian, full of musical instruments, photos, and a great inherited sense of familial pride.

Ives's father was a stern musician with a big heart. He played several instruments, led local choruses and bands (one of which was lauded by General Grant, addressing Abraham Lincoln, as New England's best), and taught private lessons out of his home. In New England's most musical city, George Ives was the pacesetter. The trueness of his ear (likely he had, as Ives did, perfect pitch, the ability to recognize each note by name without the aid of an instrument) made leading less-than-stellar amateur choruses a somewhat painful experience, but the fatherliness of his spirit made him love the wrong notes his friends sang as much as he loved the right ones—he even invented a slide trumpet specifically to be able to follow the meandering pitch and warble of his unpolished musical flock.

"Once a nice young man," Ives wrote, "(his musical sense having been limited by three years' intensive study at the Boston Conservatory) said to Father: 'How can you stand to hear old John Bell sing?' as he used to at camp meetings. Father said, 'He is a supreme musician.' The young man (nice and educated) was horrified—'Why, he sings off the key, the wrong notes and everything—and that horrible, raucous voice—and he bellows out and hits notes no one else does—it's awful!' Father said, 'Watch him closely and reverently, look into his face and hear the music of the ages. Don't pay too much attention to the sounds—if you do, you may miss the music. You won't get a wild, heroic ride to heaven on pretty little sounds.'" It was in this spirit that little Charlie's musical training began.

Among Ives's earliest memories, as the composer recounted to Henry Cowell, was a huge storm:

> Papa is standing in the back garden in the middle of a thun-
> derstorm, listening to the ringing of the bell from the congre-
> gational church next door. Papa runs inside to the piano and
> tries to make the sound, but he can't find the notes to make
> the piano sound like the bell. With growing exasperation he
> runs outside over and over again, listening hard, trying again
> and again to find it on the piano, and Mama shouting at Papa
> for his foolishness.

It was after this that George Ives began his experiments with the notes in between the piano keys, detuning just about anything he could to suit his flawless but unconventional ear. "Everything in life is relative," he said. "Nothing but fools and taxes are absolute." The compositions of Charles Ives, as rooted in nostalgia and childhood as they would come to be, would be full of meaningfully placed bells.

In his *Memos,* a collection of jottings published posthumously, Ives had this to say about the deep impressions his father left on him:

> What my father did for me was not only in his teaching, on the technical side etc., but in his influence, his personality, character, and open-mindedness, and his remarkable understanding of the ways of a boy's heart and mind. He had a remarkable talent for music and for the nature of music and sound, and also a philosophy of music that was unusual. Besides starting my music lessons when I was five years old, and keeping me at music in many ways until he died, with the best teaching a boy could have, Father knew (and filled me up with) Bach and the best of classical music, and the study of harmony and counterpoint etc., and musical history. Above all this, he kept my interest and encouraged my open-mindedness in all matters that needed it in any way.

For instance, he thought that man as a rule didn't use the faculties that the Creator had given him hard enough. I couldn't have been over ten years old when he would occasionally have us sing, for instance, a tune like "Swanee River" in the key of E-flat, but play the accompaniment in the key of C. This was to stretch our ears and strengthen our musical minds, so that they could learn to use and translate things that might be used and translated (in the art of music) more than they had been. In this instance, I don't think he had the possibility of polytonality in composition in mind, as much as to encourage the use of the ears—and for them and the mind to think for themselves and be more independent—in other words, not to be too dependent upon customs and habits.

Young Charlie went on to be something of a star pupil at the New Street Public School, an athletic, bright, somewhat cantankerous little boy—one who devoured music, practicing the piano and organ with fierce diligence. He played concerts, church services, and even tried his hand at composing a bit, writing a "Schoolboy March" just before his twelfth birthday. Ives had a number of teachers (one of whom got the boot after confessing to the budding organist's father that he found Rossini and Meyerbeer better composers than Wagner—it certainly is easy to trace where Ives's no-holds-barred, incisive opining came from) and progressed at an impressive rate, usually toiling at his instruments for four hours a day or more.

His early compositions came a few years later, mostly laments for pets who had passed into the great beyond—including "Slow March," which features a quotation from Handel, and was a piece Ives thought highly enough of to include in his published song anthology later in life. He also wrote *Holiday Quickstep*, which really is his "Opus 1," a piece that bore fingerprints of the Ives to come—quotations, dissonance, irreverence, and a certain zippy technical fluency crossed with a quirky, unrestrained quality. No doubt George helped his boy a little.

As Ives's musical personality was forming, so too was his odd sense of self-worth, the very issue that would push Ives away from the limelight in his later years, driving him not to great successes on the concert platform, but to a musical hermitage mixed with fiscal success selling insurance. He was, at root, somewhat ashamed of his love for music, it being the province of "sissies," as he would call them for his whole life. "As a boy," he wrote, "I was partially ashamed of it—an entirely wrong attitude, but it was strong—most boys in American country towns, I think, felt the same. When other boys, Monday a.m. on vacation, were out driving grocery carts, or doing chores, or playing ball, I felt all wrong to stay in and play piano. And there may be something in it. Hasn't music always been too much an emasculated art?"

So in order to persuade himself of his own maleness, Ives the great musician took up baseball and football with a frothing vengeance. But while tearing up the various fields, he still managed his practicing and composing on the sly, writing *Variations on America,* an organ piece that makes use of all the weird tricks his father taught him. For a good, obedient soul such as Ives, musical hijinks were no kind of rebellion; in his family, they were simply status quo.

As adoring as Ives was of his father, there were certain tensions. for one, the younger Ives was a classically trained musician—pianist, organist, and composer—while his father was none of those things, being more a workaday musician. George Ives had encouraged his son's abilities (which were apparently exceptional, even by the elder's tough standards), but had not weaned the child in any way to follow in his footsteps. When, in 1890, George resigned as bandleader, the reasons were obvious: he needed to take on extra work so that his sons might go to college. In the last year of his life, George Ives warned Charlie off a career in music—the poor man felt himself a failure, and he did not want to see his son live a life such as that.

# Ives at Yale: "As Good a Song As You Could Write"

In the autumn of 1894, Ives began his classes at Yale, and was there barely a month when he heard the shattering news of his father's death. At the age of forty-nine, George Ives died suddenly of a stroke.

"Father died," Ives wrote, "just when I needed him most."

Ives took it rather hard, but pressed on in school, excelling in all of his courses, especially his old-fashioned music curriculum. But the news of his father's passing no doubt tainted the college life of this strange small-town boy who was busying himself writing fugues in four simultaneous keys, dissonant settings of psalms, and playing the organ professionally in a New Haven church. Perhaps the shame he felt for his musical passions was exacerbated by the atmosphere at Yale, in the "good old boys'" club that has always been the Ivy League. "This was," writes Ives biographer Jan Swafford, "the classic, backward-looking, oligarchical Yale, the all-American boola-boola college whose football teams dominated the sport, whose students proclaimed, without irony and often with tears, their ideal of service 'For God, for country, and for Yale.'"

But the monumental school was making a few progressive changes: aside from following the lead of Harvard by returning to a more classical curriculum, with courses in Latin and Greek, Yale would add a department of music. Though the local papers were outraged by what they thought to be a "ridiculous sideshow" of a scholarly path, the music department was added, anyway, a few years before Ives would attend, presided over by a new addition, German-trained composer Horatio Parker.

Ives absorbed all he could from the frail thirty-one-year-old man, who felt that composition (as opposed to instrumental performance or choral singing) should be at the heart of the curriculum. Parker had the responsibility of convincing those who ran Yale that music could be a rigorous field of study, not some frothy after-dinner mint to be consumed by perfumed ladies and their unwilling husbands. Parker was, in short, responsible for countering all the shame Ives felt about having musical dreams. Men became doctors; men played football; men did not write symphonies.

Parker was, no doubt, a perfect match for the prevailing attitude about music in the antebellum era of the Gilded Age: that it was a strictly European import. He not only studied in Europe, but married a German woman, and when he returned to the States to teach at the National Conservatory in New York (now defunct, but then a glittering establishment), he balked at a colleague's notion that American music ought to seek an American source. Parker thought that everything worthwhile ought to be built on a European (read: "German") model. His co-teacher's name: Antonín Dvořák.

Despite some obvious differences, Parker and Ives got on well enough, but it was a relationship fraught with tensions. Ives, the son of an experimental man, toyed with conventional notions, to which Parker adhered for all he was worth. To Ives, nothing musical was sacred. So it is little wonder that the teacher jumped all over the work of the new student, upbraiding him for using too much unresolved dissonance. He was also a little taken aback by the youngster's overall philosophy—not quite the urbane level of thinking a cosmopolitan man like Parker believed was right. "In the music courses at Yale," Ives wrote, "in connection with the regular college courses, things or ideas of this nature, or approaching them, were not so much suppressed as ignored. Parker, at the beginning of Freshman year, asked me not to bring any more things like these into the classroom."

"I did sometimes do things that got me in wrong," wrote Ives. "For instance, a couple of fugues with the theme in four different keys, C-G-D-A—and in another, C-F-B♭-E♭. It resulted, when all got going, in the most dissonant sounding counterpoint. Parker took it as a joke (he was seldom mean), and I didn't bother him but occasionally after the first few months. He would just look at a measure or so, and hand it back with a smile, or joke about 'hogging all the keys at one meal' and then talk about something else. I had and have the greatest respect for Parker and most of his music (It was seldom trivial—his choral works have a dignity and depth that many of [his] contemporaries, especially in the [field of] religious and choral composition, did not have) but he was governed too much by the German rule, and in some ways was somewhat hard boiled."

Ives did succeed, however, in finding a musical mentor who was a good deal more open than Parker: one John C. Griggs, not a composer himself, but a choirmaster, teacher of sing-ing, and musicologist, as equally weaned on the high German tradition as Parker but a good deal more open. He encouraged the young man (who was, no doubt, seeking to fill the void the death of his father had left), likening dissonances in Ives's *Thanksgiving Prelude* to a certain Puritan heartiness of charac-ter. Ives called him ". . . the only musician friend of mine that showed any interest, toleration, or tried to understand the way I felt (or what might be felt) about some things in music." Ives tended to judge people's merit on how deeply they seemed to understand *him*.

Young Charlie kept a demonically grueling schedule at Yale: playing masses, attending evenings at the theater, composing (mostly songs and choral pieces, but he had, in secret, begun a huge symphony, redolent of the reigning geniuses Dvořák and Tchaikovsky), studying, and making friends. Occasionally picnics were arranged, and at these picnics would be young ladies from the local Miss Porter's School, around whom the young genius felt awkward, shy, and reserved—nothing unusual for a small-town boy. From time to time, a few of these young ladies attended the church services Ives accompanied—and one day, which would turn out to be very important in Ives's life sometime later, sitting in a pew was Harmony Twitchell, the sister of Ives's close friend and the daughter of a minister of some repute.

As his years at Yale passed, Ives's relationship with Parker grew strained: the boy objected to what his teacher was trying to *stop* him from doing, while the older man did not, for the life of him, understand why his precocious and talented student would want to waste his time with revival hymns (on which he built his first string quartet) or marching-band tunes. "Let the stuff be confined to the mission where it may do good," bellowed Parker. "Among people of any appreciable degree of refinement and culture it can only do harm." Parker's aesthetic mission fell on the side of Brahms in the great schism of pure music versus music with a dramatic program, and though he himself—somewhat hypocritically—composed a lot of music with dramatic thrust, he felt it his own Anglo-Saxon duty to carry on where Brahms had left off, with music being pure. Ives, as one might imagine, could not have disagreed more.

But Ives, being a rebel only in spirit, wrote his pieces to Parker's rather draconian specifications, experimenting with polytonalities and dissonances in his spare time. The symphony that occupied the composer throughout all his years at Yale, now Ives's First—his senior thesis—is arguably one of the most amazing pieces of homework ever composed (though, even in toeing the line, Ives's natural tendentiousness to frequent modulation caused dyspeptic reactions in the older man; Ives, graciously, redid the work, but it is the original, "radical" version that stands). Listening to it today, especially in relief to the later work Ives would do, it sounds like a display work for a student's technical mastery, edging toward irony but not quite getting there, a working out of the ideas of the past and present with little looking to the future—in other words, distinctly un-Ivesian. But for someone's first handling of a work of any scope larger than a chorale or song, it is in itself a remarkable document, and proves that, had he so desired, Ives could have ranked with Parker, George Chadwick, and Edwin MacDowell as part of the then great (but now largely forgotten) first batch of "American" symphonists.

While in New Haven to hear one of his own pieces, George Chadwick, one of Americas truly leading lights, stopped off to visit Parker's composition class on a day when two of Ives's songs—"Ich Grolle Nicht" and "Feldeinsamkeit"—were to be performed. Both texts had been set before, the former by Schumann, the latter by Brahms, and it was the assignment to use these settings as models. Parker liked these pieces but, as usual, felt they modulated too much, but Ives was vindicated by Chadwick, who liked his pieces, declaring "Feldeinsamkeit" to be almost as good as Brahms's setting, saying to Parker with a grin: "That's as good a song as you could write."

# Life in Poverty Flat

After a summer in Danbury, Ives moved to New York City, taking a temporary job with the Mutual Life Insurance Company but determined to be a force in the music world. His four years had taught him a lot, largely what he did *not* want in the way of a career: the route of Horatio Parker, determined, talented, but always beholden to the past. Ives wanted more the story of Horatio *Alger:* a grim, deterministic rise to fame (and perhaps riches), pursued in a modest, self-reliant, self-effacing way. He did not want to create a music that cowed to the Continent; nor did he want, as was all the rage (after the recent New World Symphony premiere in Carnegie Hall), to incorporate the music of slaves, noble savages, and the Wild West, as it seemed many, including Chadwick, Dvořák, Arthur Foote, and even Ferruccio Busoni, a modernist from Italy, felt compelled to do. This did not appeal to Ives at all—it seemed like grasping at straws, trying to force an adopted profile into European strictures, the proverbial square peg in the round hole. Composers like MacDowell rejected it; Ives would do the same.

Ives also did not intend to suffer for his art, nor to let his future family "starve on his dissonances," so his move to clerking at the insurance firm was actually an apprenticeship for a career—Ives's path was to be a bifurcated one: work for money during the day, music at night. So he and some friends got a cheap apartment on the Upper West Side, dubbed then "Poverty Flat," and he set out on both paths with abandon. He continued his organ playing, and even got to lead choirs of his own—one in New Jersey and eventually in Manhattan—but his choral activities remained as conservative as any other's; he did not want, ever, to startle the ladies of the church. His experimentalism went underground, with music piling up and gathering dust atop the clangy piano at his less-than-luxurious home.

The New York Ives entered was one of whiz-bang, gosh-wow prosperity. Industry popped up as quickly as the skyscrapers, seemingly overnight, and while immigrants toiled in sweatshops and lived like animals in tenements downtown, many thrived, and everyone wanted a piece of the action. The offices of Mutual Life were situated near Wall Street, which around the turn of the century had become the financial center for America—and for most of the world. Electric lights, player pianos, X-ray machines, telephones—the city crackled with the sights and sounds of a brave new world, and Ives the musician (as well as Ives the insurance salesman) was right in the center of it all. All this optimism, the rebirth of a nation, would last for a good twenty years, ending as the world crashed into its first global war.

Ives worked by day at H. Raymond and Company, where he had been transferred in 1899; by night he wrote some of his most autobiographical pieces, *Central Park in the Dark* and *Over the Pavements*, paeans to this youthful New York scored for small orchestra. At his day job, Ives began to work directly with agents, training them to sell, while his new friend and future business partner Julian Myrick—"Mike" to those who knew him—worked on the applications. The two men would become lifelong friends.

Ives had mixed recollections of his life in the "hellhole" of Poverty Flat. For one, he was surrounded by friends who adored him (though his piano playing got to be something of a nuisance; "resident disturbances" his crashy dissonances came to be called), writing music all night, stopping only to sup and chat with his mates or occasionally to wander down to Healy's restaurant to drink beer and regale the clients with rags, Floradora songs, or marches he drunkenly pounded out on the rickety piano. But part of him hated the city—he longed for the quiet life of Danbury, slower paced, peaceful, uncrowded.

As when he was at Yale, his composing took two directions: the conservative music for use and the experimental music destined for the top of his piano. He wrote organ preludes and chorales for his various church jobs, some of which found their way (after a good deal of distortion) into later pieces—Ives never felt the slightest qualm about feeding off of his old compositions. He also indulged in some experiments with sound, in the spirit of his departed father, finding two pianos tuned a quarter-tone apart in the basement of one of the churches where he worked. But before Ives could make good and proper use of his discovery, the piano was retuned and he was stuck, once again, with "normal" tones.

Right around the turn of the century, Ives began his Second Symphony. For this work (and no doubt as an act of rebellion against Parker, with whom Ives had no contact whatsoever) he assembled a scattershot set of sources—old organ pieces, quodlibets, folk and band tunes, marches. Here Ives, perhaps by his use of the tune "Columbia, Gem of the Ocean," is writing what would later become known as "Americana," spry, optimistic, verve-driven music full of Scotch-snaps (a slightly off-kilter rhythmic notion with the emphasis on the offbeat) and jaunty figures. The symphony ends with what Ives called a "resounding discord," an eleven-note tone cluster that functions as a sort of nose-thumbing raspberry, aimed, perhaps, at the establishment. As would later be the controversy, however, it is likely that Ives added this dissonant bleat much later than he admits, perhaps in hindsight trying to pass himself off as more "progressive."

Ives followed with yet another symphony, his third, a smaller, more compact work, ". . . a kind of crossway between the older ways and the newer ways," according to the composer. Subtitled "The Camp Meeting," it is a very personal bit of nostalgia, looking back on childhood—no doubt this was, for Ives, one of those "newer" ways, musical form and function taking a backseat to borderline sentimentality. Though there is no sacrifice of technique (there are fugues, and the opening movement is written in pure sonata-allegro form), one can hear the later Ives peeking through, with dense polyphony, particularly in the finale, his thumbprint "shadow counterpoint" (where a theme is "ghosted" by the same tune in a different key, and quieter), and what Ives scholar Peter Burkholder calls a "cumulative" form, in which a movement, or even an entire piece, is spun out from the opening melody.

Ives began to grow restless at his church job, though he was performing up to their expectations for the most part, only occasionally throwing in a dissonance or cleverly embedding a dance-hall tune into the music of the Offertory. He even wrote a perfectly polite cantata, *Celestial Country*, which garnered perfectly polite reviews. It was his largest public performance to date, and he was heralded not as a leader or trendsetter, or even a ne'er-do-well inflicting felonious assault on the pristine musical history, but as a "not bad" composer who might, if he kept at it, contribute something reasonable or pretty for people to sing in church. He was being damned with faint praise. As one might expect, Ives did not take kindly to these notices and quit the church shortly thereafter. If this was how one carved out a career in music, he didn't want to be part of it. Not just the Church, but music in general. "The way I'm constituted," wrote Ives, "writing soft stuff makes me sore—I sort of hate all music."

So the now-unfettered Ives, free of his desire to create a public name for himself, took to experimenting in secret, mostly with ragtime music. This fresh, folksy-sounding idiom—one Brahms heard late in his life, played on a banjo, and fell in love with—was an African-American creation, made wholly by the black population in the United States. By incorporating this sort of music into his own—the sound that has since come to be known as "Ivesian"—Ives was following Dvořák's dictum, one he had rejected rather strenuously, of using so-called "Negro" melodies in concert music. But it seemed the world was not quite ready for this: either people wanted their "wicked" ragtime served straight up or they wanted their so-called "classical" music to be refined, dusted with a light coating of opulent sugar. This left Ives to wander, and wander he did, composing a piano sonata at an excruciating pace. After all, when one was being this inventive, this much an *enfant terrible*, how would one then cram it into the Parker-esque strictures of a German sonata? Though this, his First Piano Sonata, would come to be a monumental piece in the Ives catalogue, the composer, once he finished it (some eight years after it was begun), recanted it immediately. He was still struggling with his ideas.

This is not to say Ives didn't compose anything else during those eight years—he was always at work on several pieces at once. He had written, in 1903, aside from an overture called "1776," the *Country Band March*, which was an orgy of quotations (the concatenation of which was later to become the "Putnam's Camp" movement of *Three Places in New England*), including "Yankee Doodle," "The Battle Cry of Freedom," "Arkansas Traveller," and "Marching through Georgia." In this piece he uses the piano as a sort of drum, albeit an off one, perhaps recalling the less than stellar rhythmic practices of the bands in his Danbury youth.

In 1904, Ives completed *Thanksgiving*, based on some organ pieces he had composed at Yale. This work remains one of his most striking, most profound works, pure Ives in the sense we know him today. But after this, in 1905, there is a pause in his progress. Perhaps he had found dead ends or was writing songs; perhaps the insurance trade had sapped his energy; perhaps he needed a pause, a chance to mull and to plot his next move. His compositions were rangy, catholic (in the sense that they ran the gamut), and often quite inventive, but there was no singular Ives, no specific voice. He had crafted many works to suit others, to play with this or that idea, or simply to be something of a brat, flipping the proverbial bird to the establishment, but he had yet to truly find something that was inherently *his*. Ives, the rugged experimentalist, the determined Emersonian, might well have been a little bit lost.

# The New Life

In 1905, at the age of thirty, Ives went to visit his old friend David Twitchell in Hartford, Connecticut, where he re-encountered David's sister Harmony. It was on a sweltering July night that the composer took "the most beautiful woman in Connecticut" to a concert, planting the seeds of their courtship (which would not begin in earnest for two years). It seems only fitting that a man so possessed with chords and keys (and, from time to time, their destruction) should attach himself to a woman called Harmony, and it seems even more appropriate that the concert they heard together that night featured none other than Dvořák's *New World Symphony*. Years later, when they kept a mutual diary together called "our book," they would remember this night as the first of their collective new life.

As passionate as their attraction was, and had been for years, the Victorian times in which they lived demanded a certain punctilio, which they followed to the letter. Thus the two years it took Ives to steel himself for the declaration of love that had been brewing since his days at Yale. But if Ives could not speak of his love in words, he could try to express himself in music, writing in a white heat of inspiration parts of what would become his Fourth Violin Sonata and setting "Watchman, Tell Us of the Night," which would find its way into the finale of his Fourth Symphony, both watershed works for Ives.

The year 1906 proved to be a good one—Ives wrote some of his most important works: "The Pond," a short song and tribute to his father (evoking his departed mentor playing across the water from him); *Over the Pavements*, a capturing of the bustle of New York in a chamber piece; his three-movement *Set for*

*Theatre Orchestra* (which includes "In the Cage" and "In the Night"); his seminal *The Unanswered Question*; *Central Park in the Dark* and *Halloween*, two more short, ruminative evocations for small orchestra. In all that he wrote in this creative burst (the most inspired of his life), we see Ives rehearsing more and more of his most important ideas: the layering of lines and textures, the use of multiple keys and meters simultaneously, and the embedded quotation of famous tunes of his day.

The following year, Ives proposed marriage to Harmony at long last, and the wedding was scheduled for 1908, adding concerns to the composer's life. He was no doubt in his most fertile period, musically speaking, but nearing his mid-thirties, without the chance (or desire) for a proper teaching post or composition career with his radical contrivances, and clerking in an insurance company would not pay for the new wife and family he would have to support. Once again, Ives had some decisions to make. So when, in June of 1908, Ives and Harmony were married, he decided to make a name for himself in the insurance world. Music would have, once again, to take a back-seat. He had to grow up and be a man.

# Insurance and the Development of Modern Music

I n 1907, insurance, a relatively new contrivance, had yet to be hideously corrupted. Rather, it was something of a booming industry, and Ives and his partner Myrick found themselves in the middle of more than one golden age. Together they opened Ives & Company, their own firm (which would eventually become Ives & Myrick), operating in Harford, Newark, and on Liberty Street in Lower Manhattan. By designating a whole team of selling agents—an innovation then, before generations of Willy Lomans turned insurance salesmen into parody—the two had created something new, and something that would prove to be quite profitable.

But while Ives was revolutionizing his business ventures, he kept his mind somewhat on his music, frequently stopping a dictation to write down a phrase or two. Some of his employees knew he was somehow involved in music, but he did what he could to keep the worlds very separate. He also was concerned for his health: it seemed he had some heart trouble, enough to give him and Harmony pause. Though a sturdily built man, fighting trim, and not prone to excess (one or two glasses of beer per day, his only indulgence), he would spend the rest of his life dealing with health troubles. His life consisted of music, his wife, his office, and little else—once, when having dinner with friends in New York, he acted in a way Harmony described as "alarming" (without further embellishment), and they attended few parties after this.

At a house in Redding (close to Danbury) that Ives and Harmony purchased in 1911, he would begin to produce his most visionary pieces: *Three Places in New England*, the *Holidays Symphony,* the *Concord Sonata*, the Fourth Symphony, his violin sonatas, and reams of songs for voice and piano (among them "General William Booth Enters into Heaven" and "Memories"). Together they would cultivate a circle of friends that would come to include Elliot Carter, Carl Ruggles, and a number of famous musicians who might come to try out Ives's music with the composer at the piano—and usually leave sneering, confused, or reaching for words, as confounded by the impossible musical muddle as by the snarling, self-righteous presence of the composer—or to play chamber music with him, as he never lost his fierce abilities at the piano.

A famous story, one sadly not exceptional, involves violinist Franz Milcke, a concertmaster under Anton Seidl (Wagner's intimate) who knew Richard Strauss rather well, coming over to play one of Ives's violin sonatas. The incident is brilliantly recounted by biographer Jan Swafford:

> Imagine Ives playing the introduction at the piano, autumn lying on the trees outside, the famous virtuoso waiting for his cue with that famous-virtuoso air. Milcke begins to play, swaying to the rhythm, the famous tone filling the house. He loses the beat, trips, stops, tries again, stops, tries again muttering this time. He is a celebrated violinist and there is not supposed to be any music in the civilized world he cannot understand and cannot play. He stops for the last time, declaring, "This is awful! It is not music, it makes no sense." Patiently, desperately, Ives plays over the page for him, several times. It only gets the violinist more agitated. Finally Milcke bolts from the room, hands clapped over his ears, moaning, "When you get awfully indigestible food in your stomach that distresses you, you can get rid of it, but I cannot

get those sounds out of my ears by a dose of oil!" He cannot vomit them out, he means, much as he would like to.

The world would never quite catch up to Ives, at least not during his lifetime.

# "Watchman, Tell Us of the Night"

The normal trajectory of a composition career is that of fledgling to starving artist to worldly success followed by worldwide recognition, leading to death, but in the case of Ives, things worked out quite differently. His story, rather a sad one, essentially ends here. He did compose some riveting works after this point in his life—repertoire staples—but biographically, as he exits the world of music, it all becomes rather indescribable. There was Ives, occasionally getting a performance (it was Aaron Copland who introduced the world to some of his songs at a Yaddo concert, and Nicholas Slonimsky and Elliot Carter managed to engineer a few outings), but mostly writing from the cantankerous loneliness he chose to cultivate. A conductor by the name of Gustav Mahler showed interest in programming some of Ives's music, but died before he had the chance. The reclusive composer even won a Pulitzer in 1946 for his Third Symphony, over thirty years after he wrote it. But none of this attention led Ives back into the music world. He was content to write at home, spend time with his wife and family, and stew in his own juices.

The only music of Ives that was ever published in his lifetime —his 114 Songs and the *Concord Sonata* (with the *Essays)*—was at his own expense (though, as insurance was quite lucrative, money was never an issue). He was generous with his money, giving to new music ensembles, but stingy with his praise and downright mean in some of his writings (which were not, by any means, for publication). He resented the establishment and yet, like so many contrarians, pined for its approval. By the time it began to happen, it was too late.

In 1920, Ives essentially stopped composing. Perhaps due to his failing health, or because of his resentment of the establishment, he just couldn't do it anymore. He started pieces, but nothing was to his satisfaction. Perhaps it was the global conflagration—in 1917, the world was at war, and Ives even tried to enlist as a volunteer ambulance driver—that had sullied his spirits. Whatever the case, he spent the last three decades of his life in quiet comfort, with his friends and family nearby. Occasionally he added notes to this and that composition (he was working on and never finished the *Universe Symphony,* which was going to be his translation of transcendentalist philosophy into a grand orchestral crash), but was never able to put a piece together. He stopped working just as the world was beginning to notice him. His music was heard more and more frequently, and he wrote less and less of it and seldom (if ever) attended the performances. It was all too much of a strain on his weak heart.

In 1954, recovering from an operation (and by this time eighty years old), Charles Ives suffered a stroke in his home and died shortly thereafter, with Harmony and their daughter, Edith, by his side. He just stopped breathing quietly, slipping (as all biographers are inclined to point out) into the same silent ending as many of his works.

# Part 2

---

# Listening
## to the Music

# Aaron Copland

The five pieces addressed in the following "Listening" section represent various important aspects of Copland's musical personality; three are included on the enclosed CD. The Clarinet Concerto outlines Copland's interest in jazz; in *Appalachian Spring* we find him at his most populist, most tuneful and accessible; *El Salón México* shows the composer at both his cheekiest and his most searching, finding great joy in the endemic tunes of another culture. Though not on the accompanying disc, the *Piano Variations* and *Billy the Kid* are equally telling about this complex composer. The former is his technical masterpiece; the latter imbued with more cowboyish swagger than any of his other "western" works. You'll find recommended recordings of the last two pieces at the end of each section.

# Concerto for Clarinet and String Orchestra, with Harp and Piano

In the late 1940s, jazz had long since moved out of the smoky clubs and onto the concert stage, gentrified by the likes of famous bandleaders such as Woody Herman and Benny Goodman, who themselves, being classically trained musicians, crossed boundaries by commissioning "real" composers (read: those rooted primarily in the Western tradition) to write pieces for them. Copland was asked by both Herman and Goodman to write a concerto, and the composer obliged the latter, creating a true concerto (which is usually a dramatic form cast for soloist and orchestra) in Goodman's language and image.

The work itself plays on the peripatetic personality of its dedicatee, allowing its soloist to be soulful, brash, hot, pensive, and to display technical wizardry, all within a taut, eventful piece that comes in at just under eighteen minutes. Cast in two movements (though not labeled, or even separated, in the score), the larger form might best be labeled as a simple AB structure, in this case: slow–fast. Overall, a Satie-like simplicity gives way to a frenetic jazz wallop, one full of "Charleston rhythms, boogie-woogie, and Brazilian folk tunes," according to the composer. These large sections are linked by a cadenza (in which a soloist plays unaccompanied by the orchestra, usually made—or, in earlier times, improvised—with the intention of a display of virtuosity), which introduces many of the tunes to come.

The opening melody is as soulful and gorgeous a thing as Copland ever wrote, and it is done with the utmost simplicity—at least on the surface. It begins in the unadorned, unassuming key of C major, and is in the waltz-like 3/4 time, something of an anomaly for this composer. He does change the key, but his modulations are so subtle and graceful that they are difficult to hear—they don't set the ear in any odd way.

The cadenza starts lushly (at around 6:30), but gets progressively more rip-roaring, leading (after a fantastic run-up to a piercing held note) into the fast movement, which begins with a spectacular sonority at 8:50. Copland has saved the use of the piano until this moment, the very first measures of the second movement, and here applies it—along with the harp—toward an unearthly-sounding two-step, almost like that of an off-kilter saloon piano, letting the listener know that the placidity and calm of the first section are indeed over.

The fast movement has a sort of zany ebb and flow to it, and Copland knows when to back off and when to attack full bore. The part he marked "with humor, relaxed"—at 12:00— is the most direct mimic of straight-up jazz music, as the group thins out to just a single slapping, walking bass accompanying the clarinet. But he lets up only to allow for more momentum later, as the music eventually gives way to a heavy, hot jazz section at 15:26 that blasts on through to the riotous ending. All throughout, Copland tries to trip up your ear with his rhythms, using changing meters and big moments that happen on the offbeat. Though the music begs the toe to tap, it also defies it to do so—any attempt would be thwarted by the off-rhythms.

## What Does the Piece Set Out to Accomplish?

Copland tailored the work very much for Benny Goodman, so, while it is indeed a serious, carefully constructed piece, it is also something of a divertimento with a good deal of worked out musical swagger and even a hint of camp. It is to be listened to for its humor as well as its scope, and for its very restrained brazenness, as it toes the line between light entertainment and serious concert music. The use of "le jazz hot" is very intentional, almost (but not quite) pastiche, never mocking or aping, but always instead attempting to portray it in an interesting, thoughtful way.

## Some Interesting Things Along the Way

Within the separate sections there is a very strict design: the slow movement is loosely constructed in ABA, called a "languid song form" by the composer; the fast movement, described by Copland as a "free rondo" (a form with a consistently returning theme), could be abstractly charted as ABACDBDCA/B. But all this charting is less important for our purposes than the very clear distinctions Copland makes in the score using plain English: the slow movement starts "Slowly and expressively" and becomes at one point "broader"; the cadenza is simply marked "freely"; the final movement begins "rather fast," gets "a trifle faster," is played "with humor, relaxed," becomes "crude," "emphatic," is to be portrayed more "lightly," and ends "with emphasis." These words, more than the formal design, are the lynchpins by which one might effectively listen to this work.

The most striking thing about the sound of the piece, overall, is its sparsity—Copland extracts a huge orchestral sound out of the rather limited number of instruments. A great example (mentioned before) is the striking way he saves the piano until the second movement, creating something completely new-sounding in the world of the piece.

And, above all, it is his own take on hot, Goodman-like jazz, as much as *El Salón México* is his version of Mexican music or his *Old American Songs* are his own clever "misreadings" of American folk melodies. While writing "in the style of," Copland is always still Copland. He uses the energy, the impetus, and the snappy rhythmic ideas from the type of music Goodman and his ilk were then playing, but creates something fresh and unique about it— one would never *confuse* this piece for a straight jazz number, but yet one can certainly tell it inhabits the same space.

# Appalachian Spring
## (*Ballet for Martha*)

Copland had long been a fan of the enigmatic choreographic personality of Martha Graham, who had taken his *Piano Variations* and turned it into a piece called *Dithyrambic*. He always hoped they could collaborate, and they even came close to making a *Medea* in 1941—an idea Copland found "rather severe." Instead, according to Graham, they were to devise a scenario about "...roots in so far as people can express them, without telling an actual story." Thus *Appalachian Spring* was born, without the title (later taken from Hart Crane's poem "The Dance") or even a specific dramatic plan.

"After Martha gave me this bare outline," said Copland, "I knew certain crucial things—that it had to do with the pioneer American spirit, with youth and spring, with optimism and hope. I thought about that in combination with Martha's own personality, her talents as a dancer, what she gave off, and the basic simplicity of her art." So Copland decided to make his music, scored for a small chamber ensemble (an excellent example of his thrift and upright practicality), after the fashion of her singular art. "Her dance style," he said, "is seemingly—but only seemingly—simple and extremely direct." And while poring over a collection of Shaker tunes, he found a perfectly descriptive (to the point of being axiomatic) song that outlined their collective artistic aims: "The Gift to Be Simple." The whole score sounds like one big folk tune, or at least many of the tunes sound so anthropologically American that it might indeed be shocking to know that Copland used just one found object; the rest, pure invention.

Copland, parsimonious as ever, saves the Shaker bit for a surprise ending—but this is not the only surprise in store for the listener of *Appalachian Spring*. The piece, on a macro level, is cast in a form favored by Copland: slow-fast-slow. At the beginning, a pensive, almost sentimental music is broken—rather violently—by an angular, barren figure at 3:05, signaling the beginning of the fast section. This melody, in true signatory Copland style, is played, played again with some embellishment, chopped up, moved about, modulated, and eventually calmed by a sultry, slower section at 5:17. But he's not slowing down the piece for good, merely saving his real fire for the end, offering a moment of respite in the storm, wherein, at around 5:57, a comical, off-kilter two-step gives way to a hovering, stark set of figurations at 6:47 (marked "poco rubato," meaning languorously, at the liberty of the conductor—not in strict time). Before taking off again into a jaunty, cowboy-like tune at 9:33 (the most overtly "folksy" bit thus far), Copland touches briefly on his opening sonority, almost like a gentle reminder of where you have been—and perhaps where you are heading—before taking off on a fantastical flight across the plains.

Most fascinating is how effortlessly Copland glides between musics, even when he is being overt or sudden: when the lethargic opening music gives way to the briskness to follow, it never feels jarring or contrived. The same is true of the seamless dovetail (once again, through touching on the opening briefly at around 12:46) into the most rhythmically confounding section at 12:59—even though it's sudden, it feels appropriate and organically derived.

After what we think is the climax of the piece, an energetic ebb and flow, hard hammer blows coming out of repeated notes giving way to more chopped-up figures that defy the listener to follow the beat, Copland once again calms us down with a lilt-ing violin solo at 16:00, a completely novel sound in this piece thus far. It would not be unwise to think that he is wrapping up, leaving us where we began, with quiet, pensive music. And he does, once again, deliver the opening goods to us, but in a fake-out that was the watchword of Brahms; he surprises yet again, offering the moment the piece has been waiting for: the incorporation of "The Gift to Be Simple." In the concert version found on this disc, there is a series of six variations on the tune, ranging from simple and spry (18:38 and 19:11) to somewhat dark and rich (19:36, a true cowboyish version) to forthright and soaring (20:14). Just when you think Copland has exhausted the tune for all it is worth, he comes around with another way to hear it, another clever invention, which, like the work as a whole, is simple on the surface but substantive beneath.

Not to disappoint, he ends where we began, though not in the key of A major but in C major, the "simplest" (read: most unadorned) of all tonalities.

## What Does the Piece Set Out to Accomplish?

*Appalachian Spring* is a piece of pure Americana, written during the darkest days of the Second World War when fervent patri-otic zeal was the flavor of the time. It is hardly a dog and pony show for the home team, however, but an overt statement "for the people" by a composer whose primary aim was always communication and direct appeal. To listen to it in light of the great German masterworks that filled concert programs then (and still do) is to do the piece a disservice; to listen to it as an American overstatement, one might hear its singular marriage of complexities and simplicities in a different light.

And one thing that is important to remember: this is, in fact, a ballet. Copland, when preparing concert versions of the work, excised a certain amount (particularly some fascinating proto-minimalist music toward the end) to create a version that worked on the concert platform rather than on the stage. The piece, however, was composed with dancing in mind, and ought to be listened to as such. It is a shame that we know this work (as we do *The Rite of Spring* and *Romeo and Juliet*) more as a concert work, because it does do it a slight wrong. The idea of this piece is music that is for use, filling a certain purpose, while, ostensibly, working on its own terms as well. It is programmatic, being for the dance, but without the story the piece—especially the Suite—hangs together rather well.

## Some Interesting Things Along the Way

Though this is Copland's most beloved piece—or one of them, at least—perhaps due to its "cowboy" aesthetic, it is by no means just that. Two aspects are probably most fascinating from a compositional standpoint: its fluidity and its scoring. All good music has a certain inevitability about it. Leonard Bernstein, when trying to suss out why Beethoven was as good as he was, simply said, "... he knew what note to write next." The same is true of Copland, and this piece is a thrilling example.

The intrusion of the fast music at the beginning is not jarring, but beautiful (and necessary); the way the piece careens from tempo to tempo in the fast middle section is so natural as to appear easy, a seamlessness that was hard earned. When the composer touches on the opening, as he does many times throughout, it always sounds fresh. With his usual compositional restraint, Copland maximizes his material, developing things with grace and subtlety—not easy to do with the scenario he was given.

If you are listening to the original chamber version, which Copland was forced to write (as composers often are) due to financial strictures, what is remarkable is how orchestral it sounds; if you are listening to the later, orchestral version, what is exceptionally stunning is how lacking in bombast it is—Copland never overdoes his scoring, but rather creates huge sounds with a particularly light touch. And in both versions his use of the piano is spare and appropriate: he uses it as one ought to in an orchestra—as a percussion instrument. It is always for color, never for content, and that helps to give *Appalachian Spring* its sweet, flowing sound, often imitated but never really duplicated, even by its composer. The incorporation of "Simple Gifts" seems an unpredictable yet welcome surprise, and all six of his variations are so remarkably different, and flow into one another with such straightforwardness that they never seem hackneyed or trite. It is one of the most moving examples of the inclusion of folk music in the entire repertoire.

# El Salón México

It is interesting to imagine the young Aaron Copland on tour in Mexico, wandering into a drinking hall and being sparked not only by the tunes the local *musicos* were playing (slightly drunk, perhaps) but by the overall boozy atmosphere of the place. How long did he stay to listen? Did he, at any point, ask the performers any specifics about the tunes? Did he dare to dance the native dances?

He sets the scene himself rather nicely:

> *El Salón México* had been "in the works" since my first trip to Mexico in 1932 when I came away from that colorful dance hall in Mexico City with Chávez. I had read about the hall for the first time in a guidebook about tourist entertainment: "Harlem type night-club for people dressed in your way, one for people dressed in overalls but shod, and one for the barefoot." A sign on the wall of the dance hall read: "Please don't throw lighted cigarette butts on the floor so the ladies don't burn their feet." A guard, stationed at the bottom of the steps leading to the three halls, would nonchalantly frisk you as you started up the stairs to be sure you had checked your "artillery" at the door and to collect the one peso charged for admittance to any of the three halls.

And his reaction to *how* one ought to translate the local musical sounds he heard into a concert piece is also very telling:

> It wasn't so much the music or the dances that attracted me as the spirit of the place. In some inexplicable way, while milling about in those crowded halls, I felt a live contact with the Mexican "people"—that electric sense one gets

sometimes in far-off places, of suddenly knowing the essence of a people—their humanity, their shyness, their dignity and unique charm. I remember quite well that it was at such a moment I conceived of composing a piece about Mexico and naming it El Salón México.

So, with the spirit of a people and place in mind, Copland began casting about for musical material he could twist into his own special type of composition. "After all," said Copland, "Chabrier and Debussy didn't hesitate to help themselves to the melodic riches of Spain." He intended not just to quote, but to ". . . heighten without in any way falsifying the natural simplicity of Mexican tunes."

Working from a collection of published folk songs, Copland chose the simple tune "El Mosco" to quote, but there were others from which some of his material was derived. He wanted not to simply rehash the songs, but to commingle them, chopping them up and spreading them out throughout the piece, applying the usual Copland rhythmic procedures wherein the toe *longs* to tap along, but is always frustrated by the metric flummery and tricky tempo changes. In short, he makes these "simple" tunes sound both bare and yet, just beneath the surface, part of an intricate musical texture.

The opening "crash" of the piece is straight-up and simple, an outlined G major chord in the melody, but things slow down quickly (at around 0:31) as the sway of a trumpeted melody quickly gives us the sense of the after-hours, drunken atmosphere of the dance hall. At 1:35, we hear "El Mosca" for the first time, albeit with harmonizations that are pure Copland: it is a sexy, jaunty little tune, one that Copland himself might have written. And he goes on to embellish it in his own repetitive-without-repetition way.

Lovers of Bugs Bunny cartoons will recognize what happens at around 2:21 as the music Bugs dances to—with the poor hapless bull in the Spanish arena—in so many Warner Brothers Saturday morning offerings. It is lively and bouncy, like a calmed down Mexican jumping bean, but again, the rhythmic games Copland plays with the material (and your expectations as a listener) make the section sound anything but typical.

The piece then gets simply gorgeous, with beautiful, subtle string chords making the tune, once spry and adorably chirpy, now suddenly profound and languorous—that is, until Copland picks up the pace (as promised by the opening motto) at 3:32. Again, attempts to clap or tap along will prove futile—he's sped it up, but also mixed it up as well. By 4:45, the "Bugs Bunny" material from above is now blazing in the trumpets (Copland's favorite instrument and as essential to a mariachi sound as a clarinet is to Klezmer), with huge bass drum hits—almost laugh-out-loud funny—interspersed. It grows and grows until, at 5:09, a single held note on the trumpet gives way to the opening motif, the first time it's been played since the piece began. One huge crash follows another, until, at 5:30, the piece calms again with Copland's usual proportional mastery of ebb and flow, as if a festive evening at the dance hall, imagined in the mind of a single boozed-up *hombre,* is now turning to the memory of the attractive woman he danced with or the first love he lost.

The music doesn't stay calm for long: as if in a whirl, at 6:35 a clarinet sends the piece sailing into a quick section—very brief—which then calms as quickly as it came, drifting off yet again to slow, pretty music, and then at 7:48, heading into yet another brisk section. Here, at 8:34, Copland gets *seriously* Mexican, calling in the score for a scraped *guiro,* a native percussion instrument. The music builds and swells to a fevered pitch, until, at 9:32, the orchestral sound becomes massive and thrilling, as if our lone late-night dancer is having some sweet, grand illusions.

Eventually, at 10:20, the huge trumpet and bass drum music we heard at 4:45 returns, and from here until the end Copland pulls out all the stops, building to a frenzy, and, at 11:15 there is a last touching on the opening idea, the splayed-out G major chord, and the whole enterprise comes crashing down on a huge, clownish bass drum wallop—as if our drunken dancer has, in fact, collapsed on the floor from the evening's debauchery.

## What Does the Piece Set Out to Accomplish?

Copland lays out his plan of action in a very precise way: he wants to make a piece that, in just under twelve minutes, not only captures the *sounds* of a Mexican dance hall, but the *zeitgeist* of the people who populate such an establishment. The piece is rangy, careening rather sharply from warm to manic to calm to drunk to ecstatic, all pretty quickly; Copland clearly thinks that these are complex people, not easily summed up with a few giddy folk dances and an ostinato or two.

He is not, by any means, trying to make Mexican music, to take the tunes and simply arrange them for orchestra. Rather, as Ravel does in *Bolero* or Benjamin Britten in *Prince of the Pagodas,* he is paying homage to another musical culture by using its material in his own singular way. In hearing *El Salón México,* one would never confuse it for the native music (nor for the music of Chávez or Revueltas, the two most famous Mexican composers), but rather it should be listened to as something of a tribute, an American, a Brooklynite, tipping his hat to a culture he finds fascinating.

## Some Interesting Things Along the Way

As Copland was wont to do, the opening bit spells out what is to be expected throughout the piece. The sharp incisiveness of the first few notes—designed, no doubt, to get the listener's attention—is quickly subsumed with a quiet (but still moving) tune, a solo trumpet pitted against the low strings. By making this shift so quickly (and, to his credit, so effortlessly), he says that this is going to be a piece about contrasts, which, throughout, it is. This is a piece that never wants to settle, and is always taking you somewhere new: a new folk song or a repeat that is never literal (the two times the opening returns, it is always instantly recognizable yet slightly altered).

A general point of interest is Copland's singular use of the orchestra. He was no stranger to composing for it, but every time he does, he gives it a piece-specific cast. Here, with great success, he makes the ensemble at hand sound vaguely mariachi-like. Without doing the obvious—like adding a guitar or constantly hammering on the castanets—Copland makes a typical orchestra into a dance-hall band (certainly of a highbrow variety).

One technique Copland makes generous use of is *displacement*—throwing something off the beat, or placing an accent in an odd place, a sexy form of distortion. The huge crashing section at 4:45 is the best example, where downbeat hits come an eighth note early or late, as if he is shaving off beats to get a somewhat unrefined effect. Arthur Berger wrote: "Displacement, as in Picasso's painting of the *Femme au bonnet rouge,* is, of course, only one of the several contrivances a painter has at his disposal. Another familiar device, also disturbing to the layman, is disproportionate enlargement of a part of the body, as in Picasso's groups of nude women painted in the early twenties. We have an exact correlative of this in Copland's use of the Mexican tune 'El Mosca' in *El Salón México*."

# Piano Variations

It must have been great to be a composer in New York in the late 1920s, when boundaries were being broken seemingly on a daily basis. Everywhere you looked there was an avant-garde something or other happening—in any discipline, from the Harlem renaissance to W. H. Auden to Dada, it all seemed to be going on in that same few square miles. It was a time of high-minded experimentalism, and Copland by no means missed the boat, composing his *Piano Variations* in 1930. This work was a sort of musical "shot heard round the world" for a number of young composers, including Copland's future friend and champion Leonard Bernstein, who would years later (while delivering the Charles Eliot Norton Lectures at Harvard, the set of which he called *The Unanswered Question,* after a piece by Charles Ives) recount his affection for this important piece, explaining its complete necessity:

> Let me start with a particularly nostalgic and vivid recollection from my years [at Harvard] with professor Prall—the time, back in 1937, when I first heard a recording of Aaron Copland's *Piano Variations.* I fell in love with the music: it seemed so fierce, so prophetic, and utterly new.
>
> The music opened up new worlds of musical possibilities to me. I wrote a raving report on it for my aesthetics course, and Professor Prall became so interested in it that he decided he wanted to learn it himself. What a man! He even bought me the sheet music. So I learned it and taught it to him; he taught it back to me; we analyzed it; it became "our song."
>
> This is not just a sentimental anecdote, because as we were analyzing the Copland *Variations,* I made a startling discovery: that the first four notes, which are the germ of the whole com-

position, are really these four notes (C-C♯-D♯-D natural). . . .
And I suddenly realized that these same four notes, in another
order, formed the subject of Bach's C-sharp minor Fugue
from the *Well-Tempered Clavichord* (Book I). Simultaneously I
discovered the same four notes, transposed, with the first note
repeated, germinating the variations in Stravinsky's *Octet. And*
the same four notes flashed through my mind, in yet another
order and key, as the initial motto of Ravel's *Spanish Rhapsody.*
And on top of all *that* I suddenly recalled some Hindu music
I had heard—and those were the same four notes again.

One thing he neglects (strangely enough) to mention is that
these four notes also spell out the tail of the imploring trumpet
melody in Ives's *The Unanswered Question.* And they form the first
symmetrical half of something called an octatonic scale—which
is a scale where a semitone, or half step, is followed by a tone,
or whole step, which is followed by another semitone, then
tone, and so on—from which most of Stravinsky's music is
born. These were, indeed, four portentous notes. In this piece,
unique in his catalogue, Copland unpresumptuously all but plays
prophet with this dangerous set of pitches.

The title *Piano Variations* is, without question, cleverly chosen.
The variations form is an old standby in classical music, from
the *Goldberg Variations* to Mozart's mastery (on the tune we call
"Twinkle, Twinkle, Little Star") through to Brahms's famous
riffs on melodies by Paganini, Haydn, and Handel; part of a
composer's training involves learning to write variations. But
rather than call his piece *Variations for Piano,* he chooses to call
it *Piano Variations*—meaning it is even the very instrument itself
that is being varied. In light of the pianist-composer experimentalists of the era—like George Antheil, Henry Cowell, and
Dane Rudhyar—this can hardly be a coincidence. Copland was
forging not only a new kind of music, but also a wholly new
approach to his own instrument.

In a classic piece in the form of variations, a tune is stated, run through a number of times in different fashions (different harmonies, changes of tempo, major becomes minor or vice versa, etc.), and closed with a direct restatement or a coda (meaning "tail," or "closing bit") or both. Copland's piece is no exception, beginning with a rather blunt, stark statement—not of a "theme" per se, more like of a "note grouping" (or "pitch set," as the theorists are wont to call it)—and followed in due course by twenty distinct variations and a coda.

The most effective way to listen to this piece is twofold: try to hear the constant presence of the opening notes, as they are *always* there, and to mentally follow where each new variation begins. Perhaps even listening to the opening minute or so several times over (or playing it from the score on the piano, if you are able) will give you a clearer sense of these very specific, *very* important notes. If you can follow this, in a way, the magician's secrets are about to be revealed: the *Piano Variations* is a textbook example of the compositional process. This doesn't mean it's an academic piece—quite the contrary—but here, if you look carefully, you can see the composer at work, demonstrating his technique.

As usual, Copland is extremely generous in his descriptions of each variation, which is also delineated by either a shift in tempo or in texture. The theme is *Grave* (meaning "slowly"), marked quarter note at 48—with quarter note at 60 being one beat per second.

The first variation, marked *molto espressivo* ("very expressive"), speeds up to 54, with the second variation, marked *Mosso* (literally, "moving," or "faster"), speeding up even more to 72, and the third, marked *Più Mosso* ("even faster"), clocking in at 100.

By the fourth variation, Copland allows a little slowdown, this time to 80 *(Meno Mosso,* or "less moving"), but this is only to prepare you for the quick acceleration of the sixth—to 112, this time marked "clangorous"—which is also the tempo of the seventh, marked "boldly," and a thinner, broader moment, favored by widely spaced octaves.

Variation eight, marked *Più Mosso Ancora,* with the descriptive "blurred," is now at the breakneck 132, calmed slightly by the ninth, which, though without tempo change, is a more delicate series of widely leaping octaves, designated by Copland to be played "warmly." This builds to the big, broad gesture of the tenth variation, which, at 76, is marked—for the first time in the piece—*legato,* or "smoothly."

The eleventh variation, a slow 66, is to be played *molto espressivo e liberamente* ("freely"), which no doubt is meant to lull you into a dreaminess, thereby making the *Subito Allegro* ("Suddenly quite fast") 126 of twelve somewhat jarring. From here, Copland pushes the envelope, having slowed down only to make the real fire even fresher: thirteen is marked "threatening," and is at a rapid 138, which gives way to the *Allegro con brio* wildness to follow, at the feverish 176, which will be the tempo for variations sixteen through eighteen, differed by their indications of *non legato* ("not smoothly"), "very sharply," and *subito pianissimo scherzando* ("suddenly very quiet and scherzo-like"—a scherzo being something of a rapid dance in triple meter).

Finally, all these rapid-fire figurations give way to the *Molto meno mosso* ("a lot less quickly") of the penultimate variation, clocking in at 104, but with a burst midway of 152 *subito allegro* ("suddenly fast"). The final variation, still at 152, is marked "not too fast, well articulated," but it gradually accelerates to the blinding speed of 184 and eventually to the hyper-manic 208, descending deep to the bottom register of the piano, only to climb back up during the coda, which ascends but slows, beginning at 72 and ending at 58, near to where we began.

This is a taut, harrowing eleven minutes of music, as important as it is understated, and as well assembled as any of Copland's offerings.

## What Does the Piece Set Out to Accomplish?

The *Piano Variations* are, in a way, the antithesis of the *Goldberg Variations:* the latter was composed as a soporific, a bromide to aid the sleep of an insomniac prince; the former, as a cold shower, intended at all points to dazzle and surprise, even perhaps to shock and awaken. Here was a young man—Copland wrote it just before turning thirty—making a brash statement and, like many of the forerunning experimentalists of the day, wanting to arouse the audience. The piece seems to shout, to seethe, to threaten, to intimidate, and to snarl, but in a short, concise, extraordinarily well-crafted way: an organized "barbaric yawp" from the newest generation. This is musicians' music, to be sure, but it can have an impact on a lay audience just the same—those who don't want all their music sugar-dusted and relaxing.

## Some Interesting Things Along the Way

In the opening statement, Copland uses what is called an "extended technique," meaning he uses the instrument itself in an unconventional way. A key, depressed silently and held while the same note an octave above is struck, creates a ringing resonance (generated by the overtone series, the natural phenomenon of resonating, vibrating strings by which all of our music is created), making an already stark, stern opening seem just a little more creepy: you know from the first seconds of the piece that this is no Mozart sonata.

What is most continually striking about this piece is how completely saturated it is with the opening notes—they are *always* there. From this limited material Copland masterly derives huge variety, however, playing with register (low notes versus high notes), texture, pace, and even the overall key of the piece—there are times when one could swear this is a piece in either B-flat major or E major, though using beautiful ambiguity, Copland never allows us to make up our minds, always teasing expectations—he *hints* at keys, and at conventional choices, without ever really landing there.

And yet, with all its complexities, this piece is straightforward and fat-free, with not a displaced note or un-germane idea. Like any master, Copland is able to surprise without needing to shock or titillate (in a cheap way) using empty virtuosity. And those who heard the composer himself perform this work for the first time at Yaddo attest to his ideal pianism for this work; he played, apparently, bluntly and without precision, but in a way that was ideally suited for his work. This is not a piece about subtlety, but about the stark reality of a brave new musical world to come.

*Note: As mentioned above, we have not included a recording of this piece on the enclosed CD for reasons of timing, but there are several excellent recorded versions available. The finest is the composer-sanctioned version by Leo Smit on the Sony label, included on a two-disc set of Copland's complete piano music, and a must for anyone wishing to get to know not only this specific piece, but the particulars of this composer's style. After all, he did most of his most radical work in the ease and privacy of the compositions he made for his own instrument.*

# Billy the Kid *(Suite)*

Copland's interest in moving music away from its Teutonic heritage was concomitant to Lincoln Kirstein's desire to leave behind the too-traditional Russian ballet. Both men wanted to create something exclusively and palpably American. Their 1938 ballet about the notorious Brooklyn-born gunslinger William Bonney, or "Billy the Kid," was perhaps an exaggeratedly overt mission statement regarding this "localizing" of the various arts, but as it stands today, it is a score that—even in its concert-suite version—is pure Copland.

"It is a delicate operation," says the composer, "to put fresh and unconventional harmonies to well-known melodies without spoiling their naturalness." Copland is referring here to his use of several famous cowboy tunes. "Moreover," Copland continues, "for an orchestral score, one must expand, contract, re-arrange, and superimpose the bare tunes themselves, giving them something of one's own touch. That is what I tried to do, always keeping in my mind my resolve to write plainly—not only because I had become convinced that simplicity was the way out of isolation for the contemporary composer, but because I have never liked music to get in the way of the thing it is supposedly aiding. If it is a question of expressing the deepest ideas of one's own soul, then you write a symphony. But if you are involved in a stage presentation, the eye is the thing, and music must play a modest role."

Copland said this about the Suite he arranged from the original ballet score (bracketed statements in italics mine):

> The Suite is in six connected movements, which match the action of the ballet. An introductory prelude, "The Open

Prairie," presents a pastoral theme harmonized in open fifths *[a very broad, sweeping interval without any sort of dissonance]* that gives the impression of space and isolation. The second section, "Street in a Frontier Town," is lively and full of action; for western flavor, I used quotations from "Great Grand-dad," "The Old Chisholm Trail," and "Git Along Little Dogies" (but not in traditional harmonies and rhythms), a Mexican dance featuring a theme in 5/8 and "Goodbye Old Paint" introduced in an unusual 7/8 rhythm. *[These are unconventional, off-kilter meters that give the piece its quirky beats.]* The third section, "Card Game at Night," has a sinister sound achieved by strings built on triads *[conventional major and minor chords]* and segments of "Bury Me Not on the Lone Prairie." "Gun Battle," the fourth movement, makes generous use of percussion. The fifth, "Celebration After Billy's Capture," depicts the townspeople rejoicing in the saloon, where an out-of-tune player piano sets the scene. "Billy's Demise," the final section of the suite, makes use of material from the introduction, but with different coloration to convey the idea of a new dawn breaking over the prairie.

## What Does the Piece Set Out to Accomplish?

The original ballet, which tells the story of Billy the Kid from his first kill through his death, was a direct narrative account, and the Suite speaks to the clarity of Copland's musical vision. This is, in fact, Copland-lite, but for a reason: he sought, in his non-stop quest for music that was inherently and rather purely American, a sort of stripped-down feel—no complexities for their own sake here—which ran contrary to the atonal experiments that were the musical landscape of the day. To hear *Billy the Kid* now, years after Hollywood has hijacked its very specific palette, it sounds almost puerile and derivative. It is important to remember that this is the original stuff— it is the later music, not this, that seeks to ape. Copland was always, even in his most available music, an original.

## Some Interesting Things Along the Way

What is smashing about this piece is that, even in this intentionally threadbare score—one Copland admits is second banana to the scenario—how much sheer invention lurks in every bar. Yes, it sounds like symphonic saloon music, but if one can look past that necessary conceit, there really are some remarkable moments.

The traditional Copland signature slow opening is masterfully paced, much like that of *Appalachian Spring*. With as few notes as possible, he sets a specific and undeniable mood: you can *hear* the prairie. He does this with open intervals, lots of parallel motion (meaning all the notes move in the same direction, up or down), and subdued orchestral sounds—like the oboe playing in its lowest register, or the strings used with their practice mutes on, an effect that serves to dampen the timbre.

Copland is also fearless in writing a simple tune like the tin-whistle melody that opens the "Street in a Frontier Town" section. Nor is he afraid to trip you up a bit, throwing an *oom-pah-pah*–like piano figure off the rest of the orchestra, allowing the listener to be (only temporarily) lost in his sea of metrical ambiguity. This is music to which you would like to tap your toe, but will find yourself unable to do so. Tricky, very tricky. The end of this section is a complex mass of mixed meters, making any sort of clapping along even more impossible—try it, you won't succeed.

Rather than use percussion to portray the sound of firearms in the "Gun Battle" movement, Copland just creates an overall mood of very percussive energy. Imagine this music, with all its low, brutal spikes, set against the spare, humid opening, and you will begin to get the sense of scope outlined in this multimood work. And, as charming as we find cowboys and their tunes today, the real Billy the Kid was a serial murderer, a point brought home by the seriousness of the battle music.

One of the most darling effects Copland creates is the sound of the saloon piano in the "Celebration After Billy's Capture" section. Rather than trot out an actual detuned piano—as Ives or John Adams might do—Copland creates the timbre by doubling a real piano with a high, trembling harp. Listen for this effect, and even knowing how the sound is achieved, you probably will still doubt and assume a "real" second piano was used.

*(Again, in the interest of CD space,* Billy the Kid *is not on the enclosed disc, but there are several recordings to choose from: Michael Tilson Thomas's energetic tour on his* Copland the Populist *recording (which also has the complete score, not just the concert suite, of* Appalachian Spring*); Leonards Slatkin's paced but energetic reading; Leonard Bernstein's legendary vivification; Eugene Ormandy's quirky, lickety-split–like performance; several of Copland's own readings.*

# Charles Ives

The pieces annotated herewith were selected because they effectively sum up the omnifarious musical personalities that are lodged within this single composer, some of which are included on the enclosed CD. Others will require other recordings (or, optimally, live performances whenever possible). *The Unanswered Question* is typical of Ives at his most searching, addressing a complex philosophical idea with a rather simple (but also rather fetching) musical idea. "Memories" shows Ives at his most nostalgic, writing one of his successfully lyrical melodies, and at his most perverse, pitting two opposing musics against each other for effect. At his most spiritual, Ives writes a piece like "General William Booth Enters into Heaven," zealotry and conviction at its most complicated. "Putnam's Camp," the second movement of *Three Places in New England,* displays Ives the trickster of memory, a place where he rehearses his own nostalgic recollections of the less-than-stellar music-making he heard in his mythologized youth. Though not on the enclosed CD, the *Concord Sonata,* while it can be approached merely on a philosophical level, read rather than heard, does, as a piece of music, demand a long listen, and so recordings are recommended at the end of the chapter.

# The Unanswered Question

In a way, this work is simultaneously Ives's most complicated
and his simplest. The "question" it begs is ambiguous (though
Leonard Bernstein thought the query to be, in the abstract,
"Whither Music?"). The answer, or lack thereof, is pretty
plain. Simply put, this is Ives's version of a philosophical novel
in a sigh, a quick, simple work that outlines his entire musical
ethos in a single bound. To listen to this music as anything aside
from a credo is to miss its point entirely.

There are three rather obvious layers: the strings, the trumpet, and the woodwinds. The strings, to Ives, represented "the
silences of the Druids, who know, see, and hear nothing"; the
trumpet, a solo instrument (against two separate groups), poses
"the perennial question of existence"; the woodwinds, a team
of "fighting answerers," respond in kind (or not so kind, as the
case may be), perhaps sibyls, perhaps banshees, perhaps sooth-
sayers. In Ives's brief program (or "cosmic drama," as he called
it), the characters are clearly sketched and the plot presented
in a straightforward, audience-friendly way.

The program is simple. Over a cyclical, repeating—and
very tonal—string sequence, a lone trumpeter asks his question six times—the first being at 1:25. Is he playing taps? Is he
heralding a revolution? Is he simply sitting atop a mountaintop,
contemplating the vastness of the universe, and somehow eking
out his subdued question, a prayer of sorts? Ives isn't clear on
this, and frankly it doesn't matter—in the mind of the listener,
these are all valid ideas. The first five times the question is
asked, it is more and more aggressively answered by a klatch of
peripatetic, wildly dissonant woodwinds that respond for the

first time at 1:53 (flutes, for the most part, but Ives is unspecific in his score), perhaps demons, perhaps tortured souls, perhaps the fear of the future. For each equally plaintive asking, the "answer" taunts the lone bugler more and more, until finally on the sixth question, occurring at 5:42, the wild ones have gone mute, leaving nothing but the silence of the Druids from 6:00 until the end shortly thereafter. It outlines, perhaps, the turning of the Earth, the infinite horizon—nothing and everything

## What Does the Piece Set Out to Accomplish?

Even though there is no text, this is a piece that is about its own plot, so to listen without it is to totally miss the point. The great schism of the late nineteenth century was between pro-grammatic music (music with a story or that depicts something aside from itself) and absolute, or pure, music (which stands alone). In a way, this piece represents both and neither, being almost not a piece of music at all, but a notated quasi-religious notion: a hymn or prayer without the words, or a specific des-tination. Gone are the "normal" strictures of music: there is no development in the traditional sense, no form, not really a melody or theme, and by no means is there a cadence or closing figure. Rather, when it starts, the piece sounds like it has always been going on and will continue into the mists of time when it ends—an overheard dialogue from the cosmos. Perhaps this is laying it on a bit thick, but this piece is, in fact, *about* laying it on thick, so to take it in on a shallow—or even on a strictly *musical* level—will not work.

But, to contradict, there is a form, there is development, and there is a theme, though none of these conventional elements function in a conventional way. The flute figure, for example, has a very specific progression: line the bits end to end, and they accumulate to a rather interesting chaos, and as this happens, the trumpet figure appears to get progressively meeker in relief, while the strings in the background all but disappear and yet are there when you listen for them—a lot like silence. We never tire of the melody because (1) it is short, and (2) it always implores something, always seems to call out the wildest aspects of the piece (until it doesn't, and then it being left hanging is all the more resonant). So listen to this piece on these several levels, and allow yourself to get lost in it—and multiple, consecutive listenings, especially using the repeat function on your CD player, will reveal much—this is music by which you can truly meditate, and truly inquire of your spiritual self. It was, in fact, written for this purpose.

## Some Interesting Things Along the Way

The first and most notable thing is how Ives manages, from a simple complement of strings, to get such a lush, unearthly sound. He does this by wide spacing of the musical registers (meaning how high or low the notes are in pitch)—the topmost violin is a great distance from the second, which is a great distance from the viola, and so on. They always play quietly, no matter how loud the goings-on of the other instruments, and they are in the easy, bright key of G major (though this, as Ives is wont to do, is not the case for long).

The trumpet part really tears at the serenity when it first enters (as mentioned above, at 1:25), perhaps because it is such a different sound from the easy-on-the-ears strings, perhaps because of the note on which it enters: B-flat, a note that does not exist in the key of G major, and in fact the one that would cast it into doubt (it being the flatted third, which would make

the key G minor)——so the major/minor clash grates the ear
and even poses a question: what key, in fact, are we in? This
question, of course, will never be answered.

As in Copland's *Piano Variations* (see pages 76–81), the actual
pitches that make up the "tail" of the melody (C-sharp, E,
E-flat, and C) are a germ motive of staggering musical impor-
tance: these four notes, which make up the first four pitches
of the octatonic or diminished scale (favored by Stravinsky,
among others), are remnants of the stretching of tonality that
Wagner accomplished. Without going into too much detail,
a diminished chord (a series of stacked minor thirds) is at
once a functional and yet tonally ambiguous chord, allowing a
composer to use it as a jumping point into just about any key,
distant or close, thereby confounding the ear and breaking
down the strictures of a tonal system. This same set of notes
would carry Schoenberg into his experiments with music totally
lacking in a tonal center——homeless, groundless music——which
his disciples, Webern and all those who followed, would spin
into something called "set theory," or using groups of pitches
(as opposed to keys) as the basis for compositions. A lot of
questions are packed into these four notes in particular, and
Ives was not afraid to ask——and even less afraid to have them
go unanswered. This short-but-mighty piece portends to all
the trouble yet to come.

# "Memories"

I ves devoted the bulk of his compositional output to art songs (an existing poem set to music, scored for voice and piano), showing how important he found them. As with other composers, just looking to the medium on which they choose to focus can tell you a lot about their entire oeuvre: the repository for a lot of Beethoven's ideas can be found in his thirty-two piano sonatas more than in his nine symphonies; Wagner's isolated orchestral pieces, as few as they are, were all informed by the techniques he developed for composing operas; Schubert, like Ives, was a song composer, even when writing his symphonies or chamber music. So it is most crucial to look at Ives's songs if one seeks to understand the mind behind this music.

The song "Memories" is part of Ives's *114 Songs*, a volume that the composer published at his own expense. It stands as one of his great contributions—but like all of his music, it is not the notes themselves that matter so much as the impetus, the philosophy, behind the notes. Ives, here as always, is a composer of ideas as much as he is a scribbler of tunes.

Here we have what seems like two separate songs, bracketed by Ives into two sections, which he labels: (A) "Very Pleasant" and (B) "Rather Sad." These are, in fact, understatements— pleasant verges on chaos, and sad will rend the heart; one bounces with joy, the other strolls funereally with melancholy. But they are one song, labeled "Memories," and so the intention is to have two separate, very distinctive parts equaling a whole that is greater than their sum. Ives does it brilliantly.

The piece begins—the section labeled "Rather Pleasant"—with a circus-like *oom-chuck* accompaniment in C major to this text (authored by the composer):

> *We're sitting in the opera house, the opera house, the opera house*
> *We're waiting for the curtain to arise with wonders for our eyes*
> *We're feeling pretty gay and well we may, "O, Jimmy look!" I say,*
> *"The Band is tuning up and soon will start to play."*

If the piece is titled "Memories," and the composer himself wrote the text, then we get a pretty clear idea that this is something that actually happened to Ives. But to make this piece less than typical, regardless of the bare, simple harmonies and predictable rhythms, Ives marks the piece to be played "As fast as it will go," leaving the performer breathlessly lurching to get all the words in. Ives has captured the enthusiasm of a boy in this song; it takes a somewhat fearless performer to pull this off. He (or she) needs to be both *on* and slightly *off* in order to achieve the desired effect.

The next line:

> *We whistle and we hum, beat time with the drum*

is repeated twice, and after each time Ives actually asks the performer to whistle! Imagine a classy performer of *Lieder* standing in the crook of the piano, bedecked in an evening gown or tux, and whistling, and you will get a sense of the lunatic result Ives wants.

The final verse of this portion draws it to an eager, odd close:

> *We're sitting in the opera house, the opera house, the opera house*
> *A-waiting for the curtain to arise with wonders for our eyes,*
> *A feeling of expectancy a certain kind of ecstasy,*
> *Expectancy and ecstasy, expectancy and ecstasy*
> *Shhh—Curtain!*

As no child would really ever say "expectancy and ecstasy," Ives lets us know, despite the borderline puerile music, that we are sharing with the performer a moment of active, voluble rapture—both the retelling and the reliving of childhood—and that this is interrupted by the rising of the curtain, which inevitably shuts down the gabbing of a chatty pre-concert crowd. Who knows what the character depicted is going to see? Could be *Tannhäuser*, could be a contortionist or the town band—it doesn't matter; it's the feeling of excitement that one gets before the curtain rises.

The second part of "Memories," marked "Rather Sad," is among the most dolorous, dreamy, sentimental things Ives (no stranger to sentimentality) ever wrote, a painful bit of nostalgia. His text is as simple and straightforward as his music:

> From the Street a Strain on my ear doth fall,
> A tune as threadbare as that "old red shawl,"
> It is tattered, it is torn, it shows signs of being worn,
> It's the tune my uncle hummed from early morn,
> 'Twas a common little thing and kind 'a sweet,
> But 'twas sad and seemed to slow up both his feet;
> I can see him shuffling down to the barn or to the town,
> a-humming.

Where the first part was in a relentlessly bright and cheerful C major—which Ives, cleverly, left unresolved (meaning there is no ending to it)—this piece is in the more doleful key of E-flat major, dark on its own, and darker and richer especially in contrast to the opening (the note E-flat does not exist in the key of C major, so the contrast is rather striking). And with these words to set, this hyper-nostalgic bit of poesy, Ives pulls no punches: the music is as tonal and spare as anything ever composed. On its own, it would be (as the text demands) a "common little thing and kind a' sweet"; in contrast to the opening it is heartbreakingly sad. In this short, bifurcated piece, Ives has composed something more akin to an opera or the classic "novel in a sigh." Is this what you have been "sitting in the opera house" to see, this tottering man walking slowly down a distant path and humming a tune? Or has the overwhelming "expectancy and ecstasy" of the madcap memory just given way—as memories can—to a deeper, richer, sadder hindsight? Ives doesn't insult you with an answer, but leaves the complexity in this piece not to layered music but to multifarious, difficult emotions.

## What Does This Piece Set Out to Accomplish?

Ives is not trying to break any musical barriers in this work. Instead, he aims for the gut, creating an open-throttle, borderline panicky rush in the first part and an elegiac lament for the lost past, and uses all the musical material at his disposal to do so. He is trying to set a mood, on one level, but even more he is trying to relay the contrast of memory and nostalgia—how there can be two totally isolated, seemingly opposite parts of a singular whole. The ecstasy of the pre-curtain wait is not so different from the remembrance of an old, sad, "threadbare" tune hummed by a family member, perhaps one long since passed away.

## Some Interesting Things Along the Way

In a way, Ives has taken more risks in this perverse little song than in some of his larger, mind-numbingly complicated pieces. Though "Memories" is simple on the surface, it is still Ives, and he makes some small choices that alter and sway the piece just far enough away from being treacle. By leaving the first half unresolved, never landing back on the home key, Ives maintains the "expectancy" in a way that borders on being jarring, perhaps trying to make the "Rather Sad" bit something of an intrusion. As pretty as it is, it still shocks.

The ending of the piece is one of Ives's masterstrokes. He does two things that make it just odd enough to be a tiny bit off-putting (in a good way)—the difference between *experiencing* the threadbare tune of which he speaks and *remembering* it. The first is the sudden, small explosion of chromatic harmony on the word "humming" (1:54), redolent of a barbershop quartet, reminding us that it is not as simple as it might first appear. (This is a trick Mozart used, incidentally, to great effect in *Don Giovanni*—during the Don's duet with Zerlina, "La ci darem la mano," when he is successfully trying to seduce her, Mozart injects a brief bit of chromaticism, reminding us that all is not really as well as the gorgeous major key might lead us to believe.) It is a small, quick touch, but one portending to something really dark. The second is the distended melisma (many notes on a single syllable) on this same word—it goes on almost long enough to be a bit uncomfortable, as memories can. Rather than use three or four notes, which the phrasing of the music seems to call for, Ives stretches the word for an extra two measures. And leaving out the tonic at the end causes something of a breakdown in the finality. Perhaps the threadbare tune is still going on at the end? Again, as with an actual memory, there is no clear-cut ending.

# "General William Booth Enters into Heaven"

Ives was a staunch puritan, weaned at the tail end of the Victorian era on good old-fashioned Protestant values, and he never forgot it. He was, almost exclusively, a religious composer; whether he was actually setting a psalm or quoting a hymn, or expressing his own brand of nostalgic reverence for his past, God was never far from Ives's work. Perhaps his most overtly spiritual programmatic work is the song "General William Booth Enters into Heaven." Here he takes an ecstatic poem by Vachel Lindsay (who himself used to spit this one out on the street, intoning and gesticulating like a Gospel preacher) and does him one better, creating a mood that is even more ecclesiastic and a good deal more invested in the miasma of its own hysteria. This is not a song; this is a depiction of a revival meeting among the most degraded and sinister of departed souls, all being led to heaven by General William Booth, the nineteenth-century British Salvationist and itinerant preacher, a spiritually broadsiding man who felt it his own duty to save the world single-handedly.

If Ives never wrote an opera (he planned a few, but never got around to them), then this six-minute monodrama stands for his great contribution to that genre. As with all of Ives's works, the music itself is interesting and worthy, but the music's *aim* makes the piece downright spectacular. This piece is not about subtlety, but about a cumulative voracity of purpose, bluntly and passionately wrought, that culminates in a true apotheosis, a reckoning with the Lord.

Lindsay's text, edited by Ives, reads like a twisted-up revival hymn:

> *Booth led boldly with his big bass drum—*
> *(Are you washed in the blood of the lamb?)*
> *Hallelujah! The Saints smiled gravely and they said: "He's come."*
> *(Are you washed in the blood of the Lamb?)*
> *Walking lepers followed, rank on rank,*
> *Lurching bravoes from the ditches dank,*
> *Drabs from the alleyways and drug fiends pale—*
> *Minds still passion-ridden, soul-powers frail:—*
> *Vermin-eaten saints with mouldy breath,*
> *Unwashed legions with the ways of Death—*
> *(Are you washed in the blood of the Lamb?)*
>
> *Every slum had sent its half-a-score*
> *The round world over. (Booth had groaned for more.)*
> *Every banner that the wide world flies*
> *Bloomed with glory and transcendent dyes.*
> *Big-voiced lasses made their banjos bang,*
> *Tranced, fanatical they shrieked and sang:—*
> *"Are you washed in the blood of the Lamb?"*
> *Hallelujah! It was queer to see*
> *Bull-necked convicts with that land make free.*
> *Loons with trumpets, blowed a blare, blare, blare*
> *On, on upward thro' the golden air!*
> *(Are you washed in the blood of the Lamb?)*
>
> *Jesus came from out the court-house door,*
> *Stretched his hands above the passing poor.*
> *Booth saw not, but led his queer ones*
> *Round and round the mighty court-house square.*
> *Yet, in an instant all that blear review*

*Marched on spotless, clad in raiment new.*

*The lame were strengthened, withered limbs uncurled*

*And blind eyes opened on a new, sweet world.*

*(Are you washed in the blood of the Lamb?)*

This is the march of the desiccated and doomed to meet their maker, a "glory trance," as Ives himself referred to it. And the text is full of musical cues, none of which Ives ignores: there are bass drums, banjos, trumpets, and plenty of shrieking from the damned. Ives depicts them all, especially the opening "drum taps" that kick off the piece. (In the original scoring, for voice and piano only, Ives uses his signature "piano drumming" technique, asking the pianist to bang low clusters to depict a bass drum; in the orchestral version, low strings magically suffice.)

It is important to listen to the text and follow the story, because Ives is illustrating it almost word for word. Here the soloist becomes both Booth and narrator, telling, with deep spite, his own story while leading the rabble (a chorus) up to meet their maker. From the opening march to the lurching cavalcade of the second verse (at 0:53), the music gets more and more fractured and dissipated, piling up keys and rhythmically tripping on itself—perhaps outlining what an actual march to heaven with lepers and dope fiends in tow might actually be like; no doubt it would not be in single file, quiet, and without disgusting moments. A march-like ostinato (repeated figure) at 1:00 creates some serious momentum, only to have the chorus override it at around 1:21 with a slower, more ponderous figure.

Each time the refrain ("Are you washed in the blood of the Lamb?") is sung, it is more intense. Sometimes the soloist joins the chorus; sometimes the chorus sings alone; and sometimes they even seem to be working at cross-purposes (at 2:17

it reaches an especially fevered anxiety), the soloist trying desperately to lead his flock into another key or rhythm, with them failing and falling behind. Booth is a stern fellow in Ives's sketch, and the sinners, supplicants all, sometimes fail. But his determination gets them an audience with the Lord.

Eventually the fallen souls, all marching to heaven on this strange *Walpurgisnacht*, are greeted by Jesus himself, come to the steps of the courthouse to wash them, in fact, in the blood of the Lamb (to be saved, in common Christian parlance). All the polytonal anguish is relinquished as they are saved in a momentary A-flat major respite at 3:10, a simply glorious tune. But the drama does not end there: they return to Earth (with the piece turning on a dime when Booth sings the words "yet, in an instant" at 4:10—a sharp dose of reality after the quietude and calm of the A-flat major section), the lame now healed, the blind now sighted, but Booth is left there alone in his "new sweet world," a place with less sin and degradation, no doubt to contemplate what he still has left to do. The harmonies are mostly major and hymn-like, but with a few portentous dissonances thrown in to signal that, in fact, all is not well. The piece closes with the "drum taps" from the opening—there are more sinners to heal, more cripples to mend. Booth's work, according to Ives, carries on long after the song ends.

## What Does the Piece Set Out to Accomplish?

"General William Booth Enters into Heaven" is the hottest, sweatiest revival meeting in the poorest, most filth-ridden part of Ives's imagination, and he tries, using as many available musical tricks as he has, to depict not only the journey, but the spiritual anguish crossed with ecstasy as well. It is an unsettling piece, one that might set the ear in a more troubling way than any of Ives's most startlingly dissonant works, because it is about humanity and sin—here, his blatant puritanism comes to the fore in a piece constructed with bile, spittle, and hell-fire. Ives accomplishes this by making most of it *almost* tonal, close enough so that the clashing discords hurt more than usual because they are set against what ought to be straightforward and pretty. It certainly is a dramatic text, which Ives sets with clarity and passion, but if one were to take away the text alto-gether, the notes themselves would tell a similar story—one of anxiety, motion, eventual rescue and respite, but also an unfinished, permanent work. Like the most basic layer in *The Unanswered Question,* Booth will be leading boldly with his big bass drum long after we have quit his presence.

## Some Interesting Things Along the Way

This piece was originally penned as an art song (the setting of an existing poem for voice and piano) and orchestrated later. Both versions have their merit, though it is little wonder that Michael Tilson Thomas chose to record the fuller version on disc: it packs a mighty wallop, but in a way that is both spare and elegant. Throughout the entire piece, it would be all too easy to lay it on thick, creating veritable chaos and chunky orchestral textures, aiming for sheer size and volume. Instead, Ives scales it back, giving the piece an even more sinister feel—as if there are huge forces at work just beneath the surface.

Two moments not yet mentioned that are striking: the really quick orchestral scamper (high strings that double piano) that leads into the third verse at 1:39, "Ev'ry slum had sent its half a score." This sounds like skeletons dancing the St. Vitus, or rats invading a rotting corpse, visceral and filth-laden, the scariest part of a horror movie. In direct contradistinction to that, the fantastic polychord (many chords layered one atop another) Ives arrives at on the words "New sweet world" (4:43) at the end can hardly be a coincidence. It sounds positive and lush, to be sure, but it also disturbs a little, creating a chord that is just beyond our grasp—much like a new, sweet *musical* world might actually be. But also Ives, always thinking musically, signals with his polychord the coming of other musical days, aural progress in the fashion of beautiful bitonality, a whole range of musical possibilities foreshadowed in a single, hopeful chord. Ives no doubt wants to wash the sinners in the blood of the Lamb (being a religious man), but wants music itself to be "saved" in a similar fashion.

# Three Places in New England: II. *"Putnam's Camp"*

As much as Ives was a religious composer, he was also a composer of memories, of nostalgia, of sentimental dreams
and happier, lighter times, and of interestingly misremembered
celebration. "Putnam's Camp," the middle movement of his
orchestral work *Three Places in New England*, spells out almost
all things we now come to call Ivesian.

In 1912, the composer decided to splice together two
old pieces, compositions from 1903 (*Country Band March* and
"1776"), to create a middle, scherzo-like movement to his
orchestral set. (Ives liked to invert the usual pattern, casting
his three-movement orchestral pieces as slow-fast-slow.) He
outlined a program, a little story about a child (perhaps Ives?)
visiting the Revolutionary War camp of General Israel Putnam,
which is in reality situated not far from Danbury. On the fourth
of July, at a family picnic at this locale, the child in question
wanders off, lost in his own youthful reverie. "He rests," Ives
writes, "on the hillside of laurel and hickories . . . when—'mira-
bile dictu'—over the trees on the crest of the hill he sees a
tall woman standing. She reminds him of a picture he has of
the Goddess of Liberty . . . she is pleading with the soldiers not
to forget their 'cause' and the great sacrifices they have made
for it. But they march out of camp with a fife and a drum to a
popular tune of the day." In the child's fugue-state, he imag-
ines Putnam himself returning from town, while the desert-
ing soldiers return, with a cheer, to their regiments. Our boy

then awakens and returns to his family in order to listen to the raucous bands and go back to enjoying the party.

This piece shows Ives at his most festive, and also up to his most devilish tricks. Like all good marches, the piece begs you to clap along or tap your toe to the infectious rhythms—but as with all good Ives pieces in this vein, trying it will result in failure. He is constantly overlapping, tripping up, and toying with beats and offbeats, so that the general sound of a band is there—no doubt, a not-so-excellently polished band he remembers from his Danbury youth—and as it begins to collide not only with other passing bands but also with the odd remembrance of the day, it begins to grow more and more chaotic.

As a transitional moment, a link between the two pieces from which Ives fashioned this movement, there exists a slow, dreamy middle section (beginning at 2:02 and ending around 3:00), which leads back to the marches, casting the overall form of this piece as ABA (fast, slow, fast), though not without a little, rather staid tune ("which emerges," writes Swafford, "as an almost audible sigh of relief after the bandsmen have lost track of the beat for a while"), played lightly in the strings, breaking up the action. The final large section builds to a raucous finale, replete with enough blaring horns and squealing piccolos to delight even the most demanding child raised in the gilded age—but it is almost as if the "actual" sounds of a band are butting up against the child's memories or visions of how things played out in his youth.

Though this piece is a wholly original contrivance conceptually, it is still a march, a form that Ives knew inside and out from his youth. "The march," writes biographer Jan Swafford, "developed in Europe around the sixteenth century from the drum and trumpet signals used to coordinate troop movements. When Charles Ives was playing and composing marches in his youth, this music was still associated with uniformed men. By then, American marches had developed their own characteristic accent." It is this kind of in-depth, very personal understanding that gives "Putnam's Camp" its cartoonishly festive character—this is music meant to be laugh-out-loud funny, depicting all the foibles of the bands of the day.

## What Does This Piece Set Out to Accomplish?

Ives is almost making fun of himself in this zany nostalgic romp of a work, from his own self-serious dreaminess to the absolutely open-throttle sounds of the bands coming together, particularly at the end. The composer *wants* you to feel a little lost, both in the bands tripping at every step and in the exaggerated trance of the middle section. He *wants* you to try to tap your toe and fail miserably, and more than anything he wants you to enjoy these memories, ones that no doubt made him smile as he composed this piece. This is Ives "light," but by way of Mr. Hyde, the madman. Even the heart-stopping unresolved ending is, in his mind, a huge, luscious, vulgar raspberry in the audience's face, the trickster at his best—so enjoy; don't expect to be profoundly moved or follow this piece too closely. Just let it wash over you like a huge, discordant caper from days of yore.

## Some Interesting Things Along the Way

Though the aim of the piece is not terribly high-minded, Ives still makes a well-wrought composition (and like all good comedy writers, he lets the audience, rather than himself, do the giggling). "Putnam's Camp" is full of striking moments:

the first chord as the piece slows down, signaling the start of the "dream" narrative; the jarring return of the horns at 3:27; the use of the piano throughout (just by using the piano, he is saying, "No, this is a dream," because there would never be, even in the lamest of marching bands, a piano); the final thrust to the last overwhelming band section, where discords pile upon discords, beginning around 3:35 (with a hint of "The Star-Spangled Banner"), and where Ives abandons us, as if his mythological dream band has gotten so lost that they simply give up.

Listening to this piece several times will not only make you able to appreciate how subtly vulgar it really is, but will also allow you to hear the snatches of tunes (listen carefully for "Reveille") and the multiple layers with which Ives has infused this madcap score. This piece almost makes all Sousa marches worthwhile—as fodder for Ives's fiendish satire.

# The Concord Sonata

"Before the onset of politics and philosophy," writes biographer Jan Swafford, "music claimed most of Ives's time and thought. During a twelve day Elk Lake vacation of September 1911, he worked on the Browning Overture and again restructured the old First String Quartet Fugue, this time toward the Fourth Symphony. The most significant item, though, is shown in a diary note: 'idea of *Concord Sonata*.'" It was thus that the germ of what would become this composer's master statement, his swan song, began as a simple seedling, a jotting in an errant diary.

The piece would come to occupy him for the next four years (though not exclusively; Ives tended to work on everything at once), and would come to mean such a clear example of all things "Ivesian" that were he to have written no piece aside from this one, we would not fail to understand him.

And, as Ives tended to do, he plumbed his *oeuvre* pell-mell, drawing liberally on older pieces or fragments of inchoate compositions: an Alcott Overture, an Emerson concerto, all unfinished parts of his "men of literature" series. But it began to coalesce in his mind as a single piano piece, one that would evoke the great literary minds of Concord at a time when Concord was the very center of American spiritualist thinking: the Alcotts, Emerson, Thoreau, and Hawthorne. And though Ives was perfectly comfortable calling something a "set," or adding a title to join three dissimilar works into a whole (like *Three Places in New England* or the *Holidays Symphony*), Ives called this a "sonata" from the beginning, though with this caveat (written in the *Essays Before a Sonata*): ". . . called a sonata for want of a more exact name, as the form, perhaps substance, does not justify it."

Ives intended to paint his beloved transcendental philoso- phers (and their ideas) not only in music, but in words as well: the *Concord Sonata* is incomplete without its companion docu- ment, *Essays Before a Sonata.* In the prose work we read the real Ives, who poses question after question, brooks arguments, rants, interjects, pontificates, casts his eyes to heaven, defies, judges his poor, unenlightened future critics, and above all *thinks*—and in the sonata these ideas, and this sprit of explo- ration, are activated by his notes. Remove the words, and the notes sound a jumble; remove the notes, and the words are just a run. Together, the statement, in all its intricacies and meander- ings, is actually quite clear. His prose is as clear (or as occluded) as the music, two separate parts of a singular whole.

To examine the work closely, it is important to look at each movement separately. According to Ives:

> The whole is an attempt to present [one person's] impres- sion of the spirit of Transcendentalism that is associated in the minds of many with Concord, Mass., of over half a cen- tury ago. This is undertaken in impressionistic pictures of Emerson and Thoreau, a sketch of the Alcotts, and a Scherzo supposed to reflect a lighter quality which is often found in the fantastic side of Hawthorne. The first and last move- ments do not aim to give any programs of the life or of any particular work of Emerson or Thoreau but rather composite pictures or impressions.

## Emerson

"How far," writes Ives at the beginning of the *Essays,* "is anyone justified, be he authority or layman, in expressing or trying to express in terms of music (in sounds, if you like) the value of anything, material, moral, intellectual, or spiritual, which is usually expressed in terms other than music?" Thus Ives poses one of the many unanswered questions, arguments he poses throughout the entirety of the *Concord Sonata,* which opens with his impressionistic image of Emerson.

"It has seemed to the writer," says Ives, "that Emerson is greater—his identity more complete perhaps—in the realms of revelation—natural disclosure—than in those of poetry, philosophy, or prophecy. Though a great poet and prophet, he is greater, possibly, as an invader of the unknown—a seer painting his discoveries in masses with whatever color may lie at hand." Could not the same be said about Ives?

The musical depiction, like most sonatas, states its ideas outright—strong descending octaves, dense chromatics (notes that are not comfortably in any key), harsh dissonance against firmer, easier-to-follow hymn-like tunes—even (without a trace of irony) the opening motto of Beethoven's Fifth Symphony ("The soul of humanity knocking at the door of the Divine mysteries," according to Ives), which will become some-thing of a lynchpin—an outpost inside the chaos—throughout the miasma of the *Concord.* "Emerson is heart of the *Concord,* as Thoreau is the soul," writes Swafford.

There are no themes here, or certainly not those of a regu-lar sonata, but rather a progression of cumulatively evolving motives and ideas, some that dart out of nowhere, some that creep in from beneath. Coherence as a strictly musical device is not the order of the day, but rather a constant progression toward new musical horizons—the essential formlessness of the music, in its exploratory thrust, *becomes* the form. While a conventional sonata seeks unity as its driving force, Ives shuns it, even mocks it: "Unity," he says, "is too generally conceived of, or too easily accepted as analogous to form; and form as analogous to custom; and custom to habit." Ives opts (rather arrogantly), instead, to be the journeyman philosopher, raging from one idea to the next, never stopping to retread his steps or take stock of what he has done—in short, to *transcend* his idiom. He turns music into musing, fashions the piano into his own private, maximized orchestra, and even morphs the mighty Beethoven to his own cunning inclinations.

## Hawthorne

"Any comprehensive conception of Hawthorne," writes Ives, "either in words or music, must have for its basic theme something that has to do with the influence of sin upon the conscience—something more than the Puritan conscience, but something which is permeated by it." Ives, devising to pay healthy homage to the great writer, offers what he claims to be a scherzo (meaning fast, furious dance, usually in some sort of triple meter), ". . . trying to suggest some of his wilder, fantastical adventures into the half-childlike, half-fairylike phantasmal realms." What the composer has devised is a madcap, borderline unplayable movement—one without the comfort of bar lines (demarcations that divide measures), free from the boundaries of musical pedagogy or typical issues of playability, Herculean in its difficulty. It is phantasmagoric in its scope and effect, full of ragtime snatches and occasionally calmed by a hymn tune or proper (if not a touch ironic) cadence. And Ives, never one to refuse turning a convention on its ear, even in a piece called "sonata," makes this music for the second movement; in the hands of a more traditional composer following strict sonata-allegro principals, it would be the third.

If the "Emerson" movement is scored for the imaginary orchestra in Ives's head, "Hawthorne" is built for the piano, but an imaginary piano, one existing in the realm of questions Ives continues to pose. This work requires the chops of a Liszt, the fearlessness of an Arrau, and the lunacy that can only belong to an Ives: this is demanding piano writing of the most daunting variety (and probably the reason this piece doesn't get played terribly often). It is almost as if, having transcended aesthetico-philosophic musical boundaries in the first movement, here Ives seeks to transcend the instrument itself.

## The Alcotts

Ives has this to say of his slow movement:

> We dare not attempt to follow the philosophic raptures of Bronson Alcott—unless you will assume that his apotheosis will show how practical his vision in this world would be in the next. And so we won't try to reconcile the music sketch of the Alcotts with much besides the home under the elms—the Scotch songs and family hymns that were sung at the end of each day—though there may be an attempt to catch something of that common sentiment (which we have tried to suggest above)—a strength of hope that never gives way to despair—a conviction in the power of the common soul which, when all is said and done, may be as typical as any theme of Concord and its transcendentalists.

Though he speaks of Bronson Alcott, father figure in the "home under the elms," the work itself smacks more of his daughter, Louisa May, author of *Little Women.* The home described in that book *was* this same home, and Ives paints it well. In Mark Adamo's operatic adaptation, scenes in the home outline youthful chaos, all set to the background of Beth trying out one of her hymns at the piano—Bronson Alcott (or his fictionalized idea) trying to publish an essay, his wife failing at paying the bills, and all of the sisters chatting and running about in what seems like lively, loving, borderline unmanageable chaos. This is the idea behind this movement—we hear the piano (perhaps it is Beth playing Beethoven's Fifth?), the hymns, and even (through bitonality and a lack of regular rhythms) the unruliness, all within the progressive, decidedly non–New England methods the Alcotts espoused. They were, at heart, something akin to 1960s radicals, so to be too prim and proper would miss the point—and being either prim or proper was never Ives's long suit.

## Thoreau

"Thoreau was a great musician," writes Ives of his finale, "not because he played the flute, but because he did not have to go to Boston to hear 'the symphony.' The rhythm of his prose, were there nothing else, would determine his value as a composer. He was divinely conscious of the enthusiasm of Nature, the emotion of her rhythms and the harmony of her solitudes." After three epoch-making movements, Ives is ready to push the piece heavenward, paying homage not only to the great author (who was, to Ives, ". . . that reassuring and true friend"), but also to his father—for young Charlie, the teachings of Thoreau picked up where the teachings of George Ives were tragically cut short.

Thoreau himself wrote, "A man's life should be a stately march to a sweet but unheard music," so the last movement of the *Concord Sonata* is something of a tip of the hat, the outlining of a life lived in music *with* music. This movement is truly a summation, not just of the motivic material from which the entire piece is generated (though it is deeply set herein), but of Ives's philosophy as a whole. The stateliness of "Emerson," the out-of-nowhere phantasmagoria of "Hawthorne," and the manic placidity of the "Alcotts" now culminate in a slow, ruminative space for quiet meditation, like the lapping of the waves at Walden Pond.

Thoreau, who himself played the flute, is paid ultimate homage by the use of an *actual* flute at the very end, heard over the piano, perhaps as if whispered over the water. If in "Hawthorne" Ives transcends the instrument by making a piece wherein its very technical limits are put to the test, in "Thoreau" he does the same by taking the piano sonata away from the piano—offstage, in the distance, a flute is heard over the slow march of a bass ostinato (a repeated pattern). Ives reduces his entire piece, a vast, symphonic overstatement for piano, into a single image, that of Thoreau the man playing the flute over the quiet placidity of his beloved pond. We have left the realm of the *Concord Sonata,* with its frustrating limitations and conventions, and entered the musical future, or the musical past, or simply touched on the quiet, beatific nature of all mankind: the poet plays music, and all around him the perfection of the world carries on, accompanying his holy *obbligato.*

## To Infinity

Ives plays at prophet, both musical and spiritual, with his magnum *Concord Sonata* as a signpost, a shape-of-things-to-come work that asks more questions than it answers. The *Essays* are a boon to those who want to see what he sees, to hear things the way he hears, though sometimes they read as a revolutionary tract for a revolution that never came. Ives felt constrained by the musical world in which he lived, which perhaps is why he so blatantly kept himself apart from it. Instead, he wrote his music for the future and beyond, abstract years past even the breadth of his own imaginings. He fervently believed in his conviction, in his dissonances and country-band tunes, in his musings and ramblings and vituperations of soft sissy souls who could not abide his crunchy music—he was doing what he did, or so he thought, for the future. He writes:

> In some century to come, when the school children will whistle popular tunes in quarter tones—when the diatonic scale will be as obsolete as the pentatonic is now—perhaps then these borderland experiences may be both easily expressed and readily recognized. But maybe music was not intended to satisfy the curious definiteness of man. Maybe it is better to hope that music may always be a transcendental language in the most extravagant sense. Possibly the power of literally distinguishing these "shades of abstraction"—these attributes paralleled by "artistic intuitions" (call them what you will)—is ever to be denied man for the same reason that the beginning and the end of a circle are to be denied.

Ives believed, he hoped, and with his music he prayed. The schoolchildren whistling quarter tones have yet to arrive—but perhaps our young race has yet to develop along Ives's lines. Right or not, he bought it, wrote toward it, and in the end tried to be as generous with his music as he was with his thoughts. Ives was not someone leaping on a bandwagon, trying to write the music that would make him famous just around the bend, but a sincere human with a wish to make good.

For a long time, the *Concord Sonata* was all but unplayable, especially the demonic "Hawthorne." But since Ives's time, pianists have gotten much more agile, so the idea of what is, in fact, unplayable has certainly changed, and there are many fine recordings of this piece. Gilbert Kalish's slow, pensive reading; John Kirkpatrick's manic one; Nina Deutsch's pointed (and budget-priced) traversal; or even that of Ives himself (scratchy and weird as it is). This is the sort of piece that is so subject to interpretation that comparing and contrasting a few recordings might well be the best way to start. There are many ways to play the *Concord Sonata* well. Its loose ends and frayed edges are the things that not only make it great, but also make performers so attracted to it in the first place.

# Part 3

## Aspects of Copland and Ives

# Copland the Progressive

Music history is taught mostly as an inevitable chain of events: chant giving way to fugues, which in turn proffers sonata form, followed by the inevitable stretching of both form and tonality until, after the excesses of the romantics, the linearity culminates in a crisis, coming to bear as Schoenberg's method of composition with twelve tones, leading to the experimentalists and thereby bringing us up-to-the-minute here in the postmodern era. And the development of individual composers—at least as in the strictures of the academy—is taught much along the same lines: early, middle, and late Beethoven are seen as strict progress; the Mozart of the later symphonies and *Don Giovanni* is considered more evolved than the Mozart of *Idomeneo*; Wagner's *Ring* cycle is more sophisticated—and therefore better—than the *Flying Dutchman* or *Rienzi*. Beethoven did better than Mozart; Wagner brought the entire continuum to an unsolvable flashpoint; and the only possible solution was Schoenberg, who in turn led to Boulez and John Cage, both extreme. To be a great composer, this line of thinking seems to say, one must be part of this lineage.

It would certainly be convenient if everything actually worked this way, but unfortunately for the codifiers, it simply doesn't, and Aaron Copland is an excellent example. Here was a composer whose highly discernable, singular musical stamp was on everything he did, from his most "modern" pieces (like *Connotations*, the *Piano Variations*, or *Inscape*) to his "jazz" works (the Piano Concerto or Clarinet Concerto) to his "populist" goods (*Lincoln Portrait, Rodeo*). Yes, like his contemporaries, he wrestled with Schoenberg, choosing to try his hand at the

Teutonic master's techniques, but even the twelve-tone works still sound like Copland, master of Americana. He was not imitating, but rather taking from the available musical landscape and putting it to his own use.

Of course, teaching an old dog the proverbial new tricks is never easy, and at some point—right around the 1960s, when experimentalism was reaching its fever pitch yet again—Copland was simply unable to process the newest fashions. Argentine composer Mario Davidovsky, one of the leading lights (then and now) in the movement away from the concert hall and into the studio to make electronic music, hoped Copland would use the synthesizer in a few pieces. Copland appreciated the work Davidovsky and his ilk were doing, but alas was not able to put it to his own use.

The question then to be answered: Was Copland a transgressive composer? Does he fit the very tidy theory that everything is rooted in simple progress? Or was he, due to his being a somewhat sated figure in the wild aesthetic days of the late 1960s, simply of another generation? Obviously, there is no clear-cut answer, but lest Copland's afterimage be sullied by whispers of stodginess, the record ought to be set straight.

In 1920s New York, the avant-garde reached an immense flashpoint, with composers and performers pulling wild stunts, breaking boundaries left and right. American composer George Antheil rocked Carnegie Hall with his *Ballet Mechanique*; Henry Cowell would baffle and amaze by lifting the lid of the piano and strumming the inside strings; Dane Rudhyar brought mysticism to music, constructing pieces based on otherworldy precepts; Colin McPhee, returning from Bali, would break ground by incorporating the "Orientalist" elements of music from the Far East into his own work. It was a time and place for musical hijinks, much like Paris was in the literary and art worlds. It seemed people in the two continental centers were bent on cracking something open—and there in the midst of the frenzy was the future composer of *Appalachian Spring*.

Copland sought, essentially, to do for Brooklyn what Mozart did for Vienna and Dvorak for Bohemia. But this had never really been done—the "jazzy" streets of New York didn't make for concert music, save for the efforts of one George Gershwin, whom we now take seriously (and rightfully so) but who was then considered "crossover." So what Copland quite naturally was doing made for something that, by necessity (or perhaps by historical inevitability, if that's how one cares to view such things), was an experiment. Anyone with the proper training could write a symphony in the high German style, as there were plenty of available models; what Copland (and a number of others) sought lacked any kind cultural of rubric. They were making these things up as they went along, defining the American sound almost by dint of place and time—they were, in the spirit of the mythology of the "new world," true pioneers.

Today we hear Copland everywhere: commercials, football games, movies. His sound—those widely spaced intervals, reminiscent of the prairie; those surging, cowboyish rhythms that outline a hoedown or a smoky saloon—is no longer his; it belongs to the ages. Copland, therefore, actually sounds a little backward, almost retrogressive. Film composers have imitated him for so long that, inevitably, Copland's music elicits the phrase "that sounds like a movie" from students—and they certainly aren't wrong.

So to blame Copland for his own later misuse does him a serious disservice, and makes him almost hateful to those who believe, honestly, that music "progressed" beyond such trivialities as keys, chords, and, by consequence, availability. It is important to remember one thing, especially when listening to *Billy the Kid* or *The Tender Land*: nobody had ever really done anything like that before—Copland made it up.

He also spawned an entire generation of adulators and imitators: Arthur Berger wrote a serious musical study of him early on; Roy Harris wrote symphonies and concertos almost in his style; Marc Blitzstein sought to reach the working people with his theater pieces, some written for Broadway, and there are striking similarities in both musical language and subject matter between Copland's only opera and Blitzstein's masterpiece *Regina;* John Corigliano, one of the most accomplished composers in America at this writing, adapted Copland's notion that all available techniques can be used to create different musical textures, especially when they are removed from their political ideologies, and has thus become one of the most "experimental" composers (in the way Copland was) of his generation.

More than being himself at the forefront of experimenting, Copland made a musical world in which experimenting was welcome.

Sometimes it is the ease of Copland's music that gives him a "sellout" rap—even Paul Rosenfeld, an early supporter of the Piano Concerto and *Piano Variations*, thought this distinctive voice had soured simply by becoming a "populist," in those times perhaps a euphemism for Communism. For whatever reason, academies focused more on the post-Schoenberg crowd, allowing the post-Copland set (a rich and varied group of composers, from Bernstein to Blitzstein to David Del Tredici and Ned Rorem) to either face overnight obsolescence or cave in and do the "right" thing. And without progress, composers are taught less and less, so while students at conservatories today get a healthy dose of Schoenberg, Boulez, and John Cage, the only piece of Copland that is discussed with any seriousness is the *Piano Variations,* his most "modern" piece.

# Copland and Identity

Normally a study of identity when it pertains to a particular composer is freighted with some sort of agenda, such as using the music to prove that a composer was something shocking (impotent, insane, and homosexual are the usual accusations) or that his religious disposition was evident in his work. But Copland's identity shows throughout his work—to separate the man from the notes is impossible, since, at root, his work so vividly depicts his persona.

Perhaps the overall impression of the man is that of the naive sophisticate, the displaced urban cowboy, torn between the Brooklyn streets and the wide-open plains. But one other fact remains crucial to understanding the life and work of Aaron Copland: he was a Jew. Though he tackled this topic only once—in the piano trio *Vitebsk*—it rings true in just about every piece he ever wrote. Consider cantorial singing (or *cantellation,* as it is called), which is frequently a narrowly defined melodic fragment, plainly stated with little adornment, followed by an embellishment of the same—a lengthening, a slight twist, the swapping of an interval. For cantors in the temple, the singing was approximate, not based on a terribly strict notation and therefore highly personal. Even in his most cowboy-like pieces, Copland does this too, in his own fashion: a statement is followed by a similar, slightly altered or embellished statement, never an exact repeat. Think of the opening melody of *Appalachian Spring*, or the Clarinet Concerto—two pieces that, on the surface, have nothing remotely Yiddish to say, but whose very genesis is rooted in the Jewish temple music the composer no doubt heard growing up in Brooklyn.

Copland was a homosexual, but of the generation that was very discreet about such matters. Of course, there is no possible way to get this from his music, as he never (as some later composers would) addressed it directly, even in the texts he set. Just the same, he had long relationships with men, first Victor Kraft and later Eric Johns, but never really spoke about it, even in the vast oral histories he gave to Vivian Perlis. If there were any dalliances, young loves, or even passing fancies, he was completely mum, like many of his generation. Some of his protégés—like Leonard Bernstein, Ned Rorem, and David Del Tredici—would go on to be loudly and proudly gay, which must have confused the highly unrevealing Copland. But if he was not terribly revealing about his sexuality, he was also not revealing about many things that went on in his personal life. Bernstein recounts having dinner with Copland in New York. He found the older composer out of sorts, and when asked, said it was just a headache—though it turned out his father had died the night before. His moderation led him not to confessionals—either in person or in his work, even in his journals—but rather to a certain emotional thrift. He was not devoid of emotion by any means (he could be as giggly or severe or judgmental as anyone), but he did not feel the need to wear it on his sleeve.

A huge part of his identity was in being a "man of the people," a role that reeked of danger in those harrowing days when any move to make something work across class barriers was no doubt taken as evidence of Communist—and therefore anti-American—leanings. He was an excellent citizen of his time, organizing concerts, helping out younger composers, associating with a wide swathe of others (rather than, like Schoenberg, only surrounding himself with people who believed in what he did), and helping music along at a seemingly fevered pitch, even authoring books that set out to help laypeople attain a certain grasp of music, something many of his generation (and even more so the one immediately following) would no doubt find anathema. He wanted to make a nice musical world for people to live in, and sought a kind of collegiality among composers—after all, he was weaned in France, where *Les Six* reigned supreme, and he was no doubt touched and fired up by their congeniality. He wanted that spirit, that group energy, to be present in America as well, even long before he was the dubbed dean of American composers.

# Copland's Patriotism Questioned

On May, 22,1953, Copland received a frightening missive via telegram. The text was simple and direct, but had behind it the faceless panic of a nation: "You are hereby directed to appear before this committee on Monday, May 25th," signed by one Senator Joseph McCarthy, chairman of the State Permanent Subcommittee of Investigations. Copland, they thought, might well be a danger to his country, a part of the "Red Menace"; he was to be questioned, put to task in that famously overzealous national confessional. Was he, or was he not, a member of the Communist Party?

Since the end of the Second World War, with fascism defeated, America, a country seldom without an enemy, engaged in a lengthy and fruitless cold war against the newest threat: Communism. The House of Un-American Activities Committee (HUAC) was formed to ferret out this dark threat, one that had no name, no face, and very little evidence, and lurked within each of us, evil in the hearts of men—everyone was a potential agitator, and everyone had to account for his or her behavior. The telegram Copland received—one he very much expected, having been present at a dinner given in honor of Russian composer Dmitri Shostakovich that had been featured in the *New York Times* in a rather unflattering manner—probably sent a chill through him. Lives and careers were lost because of this officious gasbag committee, all of whom believed that even the slightest whiff of Communist association was an immediate threat to the country—much as Hitler felt about the Jews.

Copland had never been a member of any party, but he had organized some populist-front–type groups like the Composers Collective (in the thirties when socialism was quite fashionable for artists and intellectuals) and associated with some really avid party members like Marc Blitzstein and Clifford Odets, both of whom had already been called upon to testify. As a general rule, homosexuals were banned from being true card-carrying members of "the party," so even had Copland wanted to join, he probably would have been denied admission—but this was of little consequence to the McCarthy bandwagon, whose venom had little truck with reason. They feared public ownership; they didn't like any sort of socialism, and kept banging on about a supposed revolution that was brewing in the hearts and minds of those who wished to subvert the power of the government; they were afraid, mostly, of the tenets of democracy, wrapping themselves in the flag and the founding fathers while persecuting with menace anyone they thought was not of like mind. And they had the ear of the nation, if not the whole world.

"I understand," Copland wrote in a statement he issued, "that the Un-American Activities Committee has a record of my alleged affiliation with Communist-front organizations. I wish to state emphatically that any interest that I have ever had in any organization has been through my concern with cultural and musical affairs. I had no knowledge or reason to believe, from my own experience, that any such organization was subversive or communistic. I say unequivocally that I am not now and never have been a Communist or member of the Communist party or of any organization that advocates the overthrow of the United States Government." Copland, the composer who had won a contest with a piece called "Into the Streets May First," which was subsequently published under his own name in *The New Masses,* had everything to lose.

When he did appear before the committee, the exchange was thankfully rather subdued, with an almost jocular humor on the part of the confused composer. In the three days since the terrifying telegram, Copland had (as was his way) made a rather meticulous list of denunciations, trying to state his case clearly and for the record—but his main impression of the event was that Joseph McCarthy simply didn't know who he was.

His private diary is very telling:

> Appeared before the subcommittee in private executive ses-sion. When we entered the room only senator McClelland was present, lounging about. Next arrives the general coun-sel, Roy Cohn (age twenty-six!) accompanied by a young man in his teens who was introduced to the senator. Finally the "great" man himself, Senator McCarthy, entered. I was inwardly and outwardly calm enough. The nervousness of the days previous was gone. One hates to be thought a fool, or worse still, a gullible fool. The list of so-called affiliations was long—nervous making. But my conscience was clear—in a free America I had a right to affiliate openly with whom I pleased; to sign protests, statements, appeals, open letters, petitions, sponsor events, etc., and no one had the right to question these associations.
>
> The hearing was conducted comparatively privately. McCarthy prefaced by explaining the committee's self-made rules of procedure, which are so much criticized. His manner was direct and patient enough. (It was Cohn who seemed to be chafing under insufficient stimulus for a show of personal animus.) His tough-guy radio manner only showed briefly when he hit upon his favorite themes.

Copland, ever a *mensch*, even weighs in rather plaintively about McCarthy:

If I didn't know him by his works, I'd be somewhat disarmed.
I suspect he derives strength from a basic simplicity of purpose;
power; and a simplicity of rallying cry: the Commies. Something about him suggests that he was a man who doesn't really
expect his luck to hold out. It's been too phenomenal, and
I suppose, too recklessly achieved. He is like a plebian Faustus
who has been given a magic wand by an invisible Mephisto—
as long as the menace is there, the wand will work.

But the stir around Copland's supposed anti-American
stance (imagine the composer of *Fanfare for the Common Man* and
*Rodeo*—two pieces that, like them or not, are American with
a capital "A"—being accused of this!) caused the cancellation
of a performance that was supposed to take place at President
Eisenhower's inauguration—now, apparently, even the *Lincoln
Portrait* was subversive. Copland, usually rather moderate, was
understandably angry at being removed from the concert. "This
is the first time," Copland wrote in a vituperative statement,
"as far as I know, that a composition has been publicly removed
from a concert program because of the alleged affiliations of
the composer. I would have to be a man of stone not to have
deeply resented both the public announcement of the removal
and the reasons given for it. No one has ever before questioned
my patriotism. My music, by its nature, and my activities as a
musical citizen must speak for me: both have been dedicated
to the cultural fulfillment of America."

Other cancellations followed; even though the committee
had found nothing, even the very accusation made people,
caught in the "Red fever," freakishly nervous. Universities
rescinded offers for speaking engagements; orchestras with-
drew conducting and performance offers; when, in 1956, the
*Lincoln Portrait* was broadcast on the *Ed Sullivan Show,* Copland's
name was not mentioned. Though there were movements to get
Copland to speak *because* he was being turned away by others,

this didn't help matters: for someone who had done nary a subversive thing in his life, he didn't relish his status as a countercultural hero. The McCarthy hearings cost him a lot of time, and smeared his otherwise spotless reputation.

# Ives vs. Rollo

It is hardly uncommon for artists to have unkind things to say about their critics, or about critics in general. But the case of Ives is, in fact, a more complex one than simply the normal sourness one might cultivate after a lifetime of bad reviews—in his case, the vituperation (though only, in his defense, within the private confines of his not-intended-for-publication *Memos*) is exceedingly vicious, lumping any and all critics into a single pathetic, backward sissy-boy he anointed with the name "Rollo." Nobody is sure from where he derived this name, but he used it—both singular and plural—to point fingers at those unenlightened souls who could not understand his music. According to Ives, it was they, not his work, who had the problems.

Ives writes, apropos of how one becomes a Rollo:

> Rollos, resting all their lives on, and now hiding behind, their Silk Skirts—too soft-eared and minded to find anything out for themselves. Their old aunt (for her old aunt had told her) told Nattie when he was youthful: "This is a masterpiece—this is a great artist"—it has the same effect on their heads that custom stamps have on their trunks. Every thing *that* man did is "great" because they were *told* so when young and grew up with it hanging around their nice necks, and every thing that *this* man did is "no good"—whether or not they have ever seen any of his pictures has nothing to do with it—Aunt put the bangle on his vest and it sticks there like a cobweb sticks to a pigsty window.

Vitriol, pique, sour grapes, and sissy-baiting all rolled into one—a true Rollo (the anti-Ives, presumably) never once thinks for himself.

His most hated Rollo was William James Henderson, critic for the *New York Times* and for the *Sun* at the turn of the previous century—Ives even mentions "Rollo Henderson" from time to time. The composer wrote of him: "He has for over sixty years heard, and now knows, several nice chords. He also knows the Fifth Symphony, whether it is played or not, and also when it is played, and he has heard it probably somewhere between 365 and 721 times." Mr. Rollo Henderson is also able, according to Ives, to ". . . detect a fantasia masquerading as an overture or a suite disguised as a symphony," can distinguish ". . . when the composer drops the elementary rhythm of the valse to take up that of the polonaise." He "lifts his brow at Brahms," and his ears "have been massaged over and over and over again so nice by the same sweet, consonant, evenly repeated sequences and rhythms, and all the soft processes in art 85 percent emasculated, that when he says 'There is no great music in America,' one begins to have a conviction that that is the best indication that there *is* some great music in America."

Ives wishes for his Rollos to have to be accountable for their own ignorance, and to be forced to explain things on a strictly technical level (likely much like some exit exams he experienced at Yale)—he was convinced they simply could not do it, as they did not have the technical expertise to manage.

Ives hated the establishment so much he quit it for good. Many artists are opposed to the organizations to which they are bound by necessity, and an American desiring a musical career in the shadow of the gilded age certainly had plenty about which to grouse—it was a time when Europe, and only Europe, seemed to hold all the musical answers. With a lack of tradition on his own home soil, it would be easy for Ives to come to resent the glittering shores across the Atlantic offering all the cultural enlightenment our "poor, unrefined, classless" artists might need.

So when the gratingly old-fashioned, misogynistic Ives demands us to use our ear, to "take a good dissonance like a man [notice not a woman]," and to think for ourselves, he is sure all the Rollos cannot follow suit. "A stronger use of the mind and ear," wrote Ives, "would mean less people (usually ladies) whose greatest interest and pleasure in art, in music, and in all nice things, is to get their names down among the Directors and Patrons of Rollo's friends, and in giving dinners to European artists, conductors, etc., with more reputation than anything else—letting themselves become dumb tools of a monopoly, kowtowing to everything the monopolists tell them about America being an unmusical country, and creating a kind of American Music inferiority complex."

All this enraged venting existed only in a heap of private notes shoved in this or that desk drawer, or scribbled on an account ledger, decrying the major musical establishments of his time. But through the mists of rancor one gets a glimpse of the composer's sadness and confusion. Ives, after all, was trying to do something he found interesting, something new and provocative; he was a thorough, trained, well-honed, and completely homegrown talent, and yet time and again he had to hear that what he was doing was not only not good, but not even *music*, sometimes because classical music was just not something Americans wrote. Perhaps it played on his childhood insecurities that music was not something a real man did; perhaps he saw the potential in his own work, along with that of some of his contemporaries, to make something that was, at heart, strictly American—that this game, the game of the concert hall, was one on which the home team ought to play; perhaps he, like most artists, was sensitive, and saddened by the reception his work always seemed to get, those musicians who fled his house screaming, retreating to the classics out of fear. No doubt these notes, written in white heats of haste and fury, bespeak a maudlin sadness beneath their contemptuous, glowering surface.

In Ives's counterstrike on the European-based musical life of his time, his dolorous cries smack of a certain lost quaintness, angry gasps rescued from his literary bric-a-brac, gilded-age resentment at its most ornery. But reading them today, listening to his rants about soft-eared critics who follow trends regardless, failing to think for themselves—or about angling toward proper dinner parties populated by "the right" people, most of whom are European—one is struck on a deeper level with a startling thought: things haven't really changed at all.

# The Case of Mr. Ives

Many consider Ives to be the ratty genius, tucked away somewhere in the woods or by the pond, who single-handedly presaged many of the musical innovations of the twentieth century, writing atonal music long before Schoenberg in Austria and bitonal music ages before Milhaud in France, when Hindemith was just a baby. He labored out of the public eye, for the most part, continually worked on several pieces at once, revising, retooling, stringing two old works together as one, and so on. Some see him as a prophet, a sage way ahead of his time. There are, however, those who not only don't cotton to his music (many find it sloppy, inelegant, vulgar, lacking form or development or any sort of technique), but say that he might have perpetrated something rather underhanded: he might have backdated his works, or revised them later, adding more dissonance and yet allowing the notion to take hold that his bangs and clashes had been written years earlier.

The question this brooks: Is the legend of Ives and his foretelling the future more important than his work? Composer Elliot Carter, an intimate of Ives (and someone who has written some of the thorniest, most harrowing musical scores to date, music dense with outright surface complexity), has this to say:

> A Matter which puzzles me still is the question of Ives's revision of his own scores. I can remember vividly a visit on a late afternoon to his house on East 74th Street, when I was directed to a little top-floor room where Ives sat at a little upright piano with score pages strewn around on the floor and tables—this must have been around 1929. He was

working on, I think, *Three Places in New England,* getting the score ready for performance. A new score was being derived from the older one to which he was adding and changing, turning octaves into sevenths and ninths, and adding disso-nant notes. Since then I have often wondered at exactly what date a lot of the music written early in his life received its last shot of dissonance and polyrhythm. In this case he showed me quite simply how he was improving the score. I got the impression that he might have frequently jacked up the level of dissonance of many works as his tastes changed. While the question no longer seems important, one could wonder whether he was as early a precursor of "modern" music as is sometimes made out.

It does lead one to wonder more than that: it makes one question not only his place in history, but—if he were party to this bit of flummery, rewriting his own legend along with his music—how true his early stories about his father are. Ives's work is largely about remembering—or, more important, *mis*-remembering—things from his early childhood, representing them in a jumble or a haze or a slamming shot, and if he did either "fix" or backdate his scores, one wonders what else he managed to persuade people to believe.

So it is difficult to agree with Carter when he says the question no longer seems important, because if we are to properly evaluate Ives, who is held up as the great American seer, one who was, in his day, underrated for his progressive-ness, shunned for ideas that were later wholly embraced by the music world when they began to come from Europe, we need to know how much of a soothsayer he really was. And, like so many things about Ives, it is confounding because we never will know the truth.

He was a complex man, to be sure, this composer of infi-nite subtlety and vast vulgarity, his works running the catholic gamut, from showy imitations of out-of-tune bands to sub-lime symphonies to be played on a mountaintop; embracing pacifism, transcendentalism, progressivism, and the selling of insurance; transforming himself from a shy, retiring, daddy's-boy Yalie to a crotchety know-it-all, putting each and every Rollo in his place; shunning the musical world at the same time he yearned for its love. How much of this legend is, in fact, merely legend? Did Ives, if he exaggerated his dissonances and laid claim to contributions he might not have made, make up other things as well? Can we believe a word he says about himself or his work? In true Ivesian spirit, these will forever be unanswered questions.

The fact that Ives retreated—like American authors J. D. Salinger and Thomas Pynchon—only adds to his legend, augments his mystique. In America, we like heroes who leave, sensitive souls who find the world too much for them, working in secret on the "Magic Mountain" without encouragement from their native land, more concerned with posterity than career. The question (Ives's music is always full of questions, so it hardly seems improper to ask) is: How much of his own legend was self-cultivated?

If it were to come out, perhaps ferreted out by a clever academic by examining his sketches, that Ives did revise or backdate his scores, then what would become of him—how would history revise itself to meet the lessening of the giant? If in 1923—the year Schoenberg wrote his shot-heard-round-the-world *Five Piano Pieces,* Op. 23, considered by most to be the first truly atonal work—Ives began a series of changes to his manuscripts to prove that he did it first, what would his music come to mean?

The main question: Do we who love Ives love him for his work or his innovations?

There is no simple answer because the progressive nature behind Ives's work is not ancillary; we look to Ives for quality, but just as much for innovation. As epoch-making as the 40th Symphony of Mozart and the Ninth of Beethoven were, we like them because they move us, not because they changed the world. With Ives it is a totally different story—his legend informs his music, not the other way around. So what if that legend were debunked?

It is not the purpose here to answer this question, to root out the trouble, to smash the idol; it is, rather, to make us consider Ives on the grounds that he—or at least a part of him—might have liked: by a strict survey of the music he wrote, regardless of date, time, or where and when it was composed. Not to break him down to the smallest social bit, but to absorb his music as it was meant to be heard, *as music.* Then, and only then, can an honest assessment of his worth be made. "The strains of one man," wrote Ives, "may fall far below the course of those Phaetons of Concord, or of the Aegean Sea, or of Westmoreland—but the greater the distance his music falls away, the more reason that some greater man shall bring his nearer to those higher spheres."

# The Composers as Authors

Both Copland and Ives led interesting double (or triple) lives, being not only groundbreaking composers, but authors as well. And their prose not only informs (and was informed by) their music, but the very nature of what they wrote, how they wrote, and for whom they wrote gives substantial insight into their personalities.

Copland was a man of the people, and his prose works reflect this. One book he wrote, *What to Listen for in Music,* is still in print and selling well as of this writing. It is a basic quick-fix music appreciation course, culled from lectures he gave at the New School early in his career. Someone told him he was "talking a book," and so he had himself transcribed and edited. This tidy little volume is an excellent starting point for those curious about the alchemy of musical creation—though he was not, like Leonard Bernstein (who gave the famous Young People's Concerts), accused of being a magician revealing the secrets behind the prestidigitations. Instead, his book was (and is) viewed as an exigent fillip, something from which an interested-but-yet-to-be-enlightened listener might quickly garner all the necessary basics. Much as the book you are reading tries to explain Copland and Ives, Copland's book attempts to explain all music. He begins with a straight, unadorned statement—as he does in his compositions—that his aim is to ". . . put down as clearly as possible the fundamentals of intelligent music listening." In it, he discusses the basics of the creative process—rhythm, melody, harmony, color, texture, structure, form—and forays into opera, film music, and offers (with characteristic generosity) a list of further books to read on the topic.

In order to make money early on, Copland was a some-times-critic for a number of journals, and these writings were culled to make a book called *Our New Music* (later revised as *The New Music 1900–1960*). This book, sadly out of print, is well worth investigating for the Coplandite (or even new enthusiasts) because it covers this important composer's opinions on a number of topics, from Machaut to Milhaud to his contemporaries, including the young, up-and-coming generation. He speaks at interesting length about the shadow of Europe ("Few music lovers realize to what extent we are dominated by the romantic tradition of the nineteenth century"), the music of Latin America, jazz, Ives (with great, guarded admiration), technology, and finally, in a rare revelatory moment, about himself.

Another collection of articles appeared, this one a little less organized (but no less interesting) called *Copland on Music*. In this book—as succinct and to-the-point as his others—Copland discusses various musical personalities, from Stravinsky, Boulanger, Benjamin Britten, and Ives to Serge Koussevitzky, Paul Rosenfeld, William Kapell, and his usual gang of Latin American composers like Ginastera and Chavez, for whom his enthusiasm never abated. He also speaks candidly about his admiration for Mozart, and his completely surprising envy of Liszt and Berlioz, seemingly his aesthetic polar opposites. Readers of this book are also treated to bits of his journal—though he, unlike his protégé Ned Rorem, includes not even a whiff of scandal, bitchiness, or airing dirty laundry, choosing instead to focus only on music.

Copland's last book, published in the 1950s, is the written text of his Charles Eliot Norton Lectures, delivered at Harvard in 1951–52. *Music and Imagination,* as he chose to call it, is a more focused account of the topics that concerned him most throughout his life: composing, creativity, and the fate of contemporary American music. Here, though, he is speaking in a loftier way, aiming for a more sophisticated crowd than in all his other prose works. As the Norton Lecture post—called a "throne" by future occupier Leonard Bernstein—is meant to shed light not only on the personality giving the lectures, but also on a specific musical issue, Copland weaves his narrative around the plainly stated idea of imagination, applying it to his own generation of composers. Self-references here, as in all of his prose works, are scant and always humble.

As much as Copland's authorial output is instructive and deeply involved in his own generation, Ives's works of prose are deeply philosophical—and few are actually meant for publication. Where Copland was a pragmatic man, Ives was spiritual, something of a musical hierophant. His *Memos* were collected after his death by his amanuensis John Kirkpatrick, and as they were not meant to be read (though, knowing this composer's cantankerous, self-inflated personality, they were no doubt intended to be pored over by *someone*) we can get a glimpse into Ives's enigmatic—and often frustrating—mind. He speaks largely about his own music, but does touch on other composers: he found Stravinsky's *Firebird* ". . . morbid and monotonous"; he thought that Beethoven was a "great man," but during an extended listening he longed for ". . . just one big strong chord not tied to any key"; and found Brahms "not quite as strong as Carl Ruggles" because he had "too much of the sugar-plum for the soft ears." These prose nuggets give us great insight not only into Ives's character, but also into his work—he very carefully (though often with great vitriol) explains how his music ought to be performed: a boon for future generations. It is also in these pages that we first meet Rollo, the everyman music critic whose ears, according to the composer, are not sophisticated enough to understand his work.

The *Essays Before a Sonata* were written to accompany his self-published *Concord Sonata* by means of explanation; they read more like philosophical liner notes than a chart wherein the *terra incognita* of Ives's piece can be effectively navigated. These essays are a must for anyone attempting to understand this work, as they speak in great detail not about the technical constructions (check the *Memos* for that), but about the spiritual impulse behind the sonata, which is its defining ideal. Ives was a dyed-in-the-wool transcendentalist-cum–New England puritan, and his ruminations (both musical and textual) on Emerson, Hawthorne, the Alcotts, and Thoreau make for fascinating, beautiful reading. Of course, he must get his jabs in on the doubters he feared so deeply and so well, dedicating the entire book thus: "The prefatory essays were written by the composer for those who can't stand his music—and the music for those who can't stand his essays; to those who can't stand either, the whole is respectfully dedicated."

Ives published a few other sundry pieces of prose: a much needed conductor's note to accompany the score of his Fourth Symphony, a quick little offering as an afterpiece to his 114 Songs, and, oddly enough, a pamphlet about insurance called *The Amount to Carry—Measuring the Prospect,* which is still read today in the insurance world, albeit as a quaint reminder rather than a useful document. But he was never much for teaching or for promoting the work of others, except his coterie, so his contributions as a writer are rather limited.

# Afterword

It is my greatest hope that you have not only learned how to listen well and deeply to the music of Copland and Ives—and that their characters have been sketched in a clear enough fashion that you are now cognizant of the *people* behind all the notes—but that you also appreciate, to a greater degree, how to listen differently.

These two composers, so alike in a few superficial ways, could not be more different. Where Ives was freighted with his own philosophical notions, Copland, no small thinker himself, wrote for the people rather than the ages. Doing a note-by-note recall of an Ives work would miss the point, as would doing a philosophical reading of Copland. For Ives to create a danceable ballet set in the Wild West (or a danceable work, period!) would be as ludicrous as it would be for Copland to compose a work called "Essays Before a Rodeo." Each composer inhabits a totally different, completely singular space, so much so that one must listen in strikingly different ways to their respective work to get the most out of it.

Both composers had an investment in America, but different aims and experiences. Ives was an insider, trying to bring his America to the tradition, while Copland, the former ex-patriot and Boulanger student, was trying to bring the tradition to America. Both used folk songs, but Ives as a point of memory and Copland as an "Americanizing" novelty. Both believed that classical music was not something strictly imported for the amusement of the wealthy following the golden age, but while

Copland sought to bring composers and audiences together, Ives defied the musical establishment and retreated to work in secret. Their lives could not have been more different, and, consequently, neither could their music.

Their sphere of influence runs the gamut of all the subsequent American composers—to be a composer here, you have to wrestle with the spirit and work of both of these men. A whole school of musical thought formed around each: Copland even had young disciples, some of whom make cameo appearances in this book (Harold Shapero, Arthur Berger, Ned Rorem, Marc Blitzstein, Leonard Bernstein, Roy Harris, Irving Fine, John Corigliano, and William Schuman, to name a few); Ives, though not without his immediate descendants (Carl Ruggles and Henry Brandt), had a wider purview, and his influence is a little more broadly felt. Elliot Carter's experiments with fiercely independent musical lines would likely not exist without Ives, nor is it easy to imagine many of the antics of the likes of John Cage, Lou Harrison, Terry Riley without the pioneering experimentalist *esprit de corps* whipped up by the legend of Ives.

Copland and Ives knew each other only cursorily, and would not have been fast friends. The scene is almost painful to imagine: Ives objecting to Copland for a whole host of reasons—his homosexuality, populism, easy melodies, mild Communist sympathies, European education, and presence within the musical establishment are only a few. Copland, on the other hand, would no doubt (good soul that he was) have attempted to persuade Ives of the worth of his own music regardless of what critics said, attempted to sway him into taking a more active role in his own career. He might have even given the woodsy crank a few well-meant tips about how he might simplify his technically unsound notation, so that his music would be easier to read and play. Ives, no doubt, would have reacted sharply ("God *damn* simplicity," he said often to his amanuensis, the pianist John Kirkpatrick) and after the meeting, written a furious memo condemning "Rollo Copland and his school of Americana."

One can imagine the young Aaron Copland, sweetly intimidated by the great old coot of mystery (in speaking of Ives on camera, the younger composer shyly admits, "I'm a composer too," as if in the presence of this sort of brilliance he must be a tiny bit humble), slinking back to his "city slicker" friends, aware of the man's brilliance but put off by his loutish, macho behavior. Ives, still scribbling madly at his desk to nobody, pausing, looking up and wondering, perhaps with a whiff of sadness, just how he might get his music played more often, like that nice kid who came to visit.

Different listening is not just to be applied to Copland and Ives, however, and if this book manages to accomplish anything, it will be to reconfigure your ears for each new musical scene you experience, so that you can appreciate the work for what you feel the intent is, rather than filtering it through any preconceptions you might have, or even your simple "thumbs-up, thumbs-down" opinion. Classical music is a broad field, an exciting, provocative realm, with literally something for everyone, from the most hardcore of hearts to the gentlest and most genteel of sensibilities. Perhaps neither Ives nor Copland suit your taste, but the important thing to know is that you *listened*—not in a cursory fashion, but really took the time to arrive at your displeasure intelligently and with open ears. There is a whole world of great music out there if you have the courage to hear it.

# Suggested Further Listening

## Copland

His opera *The Tender Land* is a quirky little masterpiece (in both its full version and the chamber version arranged by Murray Sidlin), as is his choral work *In The Beginning* and his piece for children *The Second Hurricane*. His piano trio *Vitebsk* is an oddity in his canon, and well worth serious attention, as is his Nonet and Piano Quartet.

Some of his odder orchestral works, including the *Symphonic Ode, Inscape, Connotations,* and *An Outdoor Overture,* are as worth investigating as his more familiar *Third Symphony, Rodeo,* and *Danzon Cubano.* And on the smaller side, his *Twelve Poems of Emily Dickinson* and *Duo for Flute and Piano* are both masterpieces, as are his Piano Sonata, Piano Fantasy, *Night Thoughts,* and Sonata for Violin and Piano.

## Ives

His four symphonies are worth investigating, particularly the Fourth, his last, great epic statement, and the *Holidays Symphony.* His recently reconstructed *Emerson Concerto* for piano and orchestra is worthy of attention, as it is a rather recent Ives piece and has all the germ ideas for the Concord Sonata.

All four of his sonatas for violin and piano are masterpieces, as is his Piano Trio, and his first and second string quartets show a composer really trying to discover himself. He also wrote a whole host of small orchestral pieces, many of which have been recorded and all of which are fascinating: *The Pond, Halloween, From the Steeples and Mountains, Robert Browning Overture, Central Park in the Dark, Over the Pavements, Calcium Light Night,* and the two un-discussed movements from *Three Places in New England:* The "St. Gaudens" in Boston Common and The Housatonic at Stockbridge.

Ives's songs are a vast place to study, with many fine recordings available (though none so legendary as that of Gilbert Kalish accompanying Jan De Gaetani). A dip into his 114 Songs is a tour through a panoply of musical styles, though a few of them stand out as being particularly worthy: "They Are There," "Serenity," "Like a Sick Eagle," "Charlie Rutlage," "Two Little Flowers," and "The Things Our Fathers Loved."

These lists, of course, represent a small portion of the vast output these two men have offered us. But you may take comfort in the fact that if the work of either of these composers spoke to you, there is a lot of great listening in store for you.

# Suggested Further Reading

## Copland

Four amazing books about Aaron Copland are enormously informative. Vivian Perlis is the great documenter. I drew a good portion of the composer's quotes from her two volumes, *Copland 1900–1942* and *Copland Since 1943*. They are a massive set of oral histories, which she weaves together with biographical sections, absolutely invaluable for anyone with an interest in this composer.

Also useful is Howard Pollock's monumental *Aaron Copland: The Life and Work of an Uncommon Man*. Pollock is less discreet than Perlis, who has palpable reverence for Copland's privacy, whereas Pollock is more objective and therefore delivers more inside information.

Arthur Berger's early study, *Aaron Copland,* now out of print, is worth rooting around for, because, being a composer himself, he goes into more musical detail than the others. It was written in 1953, so a good deal of Copland's work was not yet composed at the time. Perhaps someday someone will do a follow-up, an addendum that covers the whole spectrum. But, as it stands, this work is a thorough technical examination of the music that this great composer wrote.

Ned Rorem, a Copland student, admirer, and friend, writes a lovely paean to the composer, which is included in his book, *The Ned Rorem Reader.* Paul Rosenfeld, as well, writes beautifully about Copland in any of his collections—also sadly out of print, but worth looking for.

And, of course, Copland himself wrote *What to Listen for in Music, Music and Imagination, Our New Music,* and *Copland on Music,* all valuable for different reasons and all excellent sources of information about not only the music of Copland and his ilk, but music in general. He was a great explainer, perhaps the greatest.

## Ives

This book could not have been written without Jan Swafford's extraordinary *Charles Ives: A Life with Music.* As in his biography of Brahms, he offers the most lovingly comprehensive look at a complex figure. A composer and author himself, he writes with equal alacrity about Ives's life and personality as he does about his music in a compelling, readable volume—a must for anyone who wants to know more about Ives.

Once again, Vivian Perlis has offered us a special gift in *Charles Ives Remembered,* a transcribed set of oral histories, introduced by Aaron Copland. She speaks to everyone from his neighbors' children to other composers who knew him to relatives, and from this a comprehensive portrait can be drawn.

Anyone who wants to study Ives and his music with any depth should read *Charles Ives: The Ideas Behind the Music* and *All Made of Tunes: Charles Ives and the Uses of Musical Borrowing,* both by the brilliant J. Peter Burkholder. He also edited two important volumes: *Charles Ives and His World* and *Charles Ives and the Classical Tradition.*

It goes without saying that Thoreau's *Walden,* Emerson's essays, Hawthorne's novels, Bronson Alcott's letters, and Louisa May Alcott's novel *Little Women* are necessary to understand the genesis for many of Ives's ideas. Secondary sources on any of these figures, writings on the transcendentalist movement, and a visit to Walden Pond in Concord, Massachusetts, would also be helpful.

And, of course, Ives in his own words: *Memos,* as well as *Essays Before a Sonata* (a Dover reprint also featuring interesting writings by Debussy and Busoni), is mandatory reading for the future Ivesian.

## General Information

Of course, *The New Grove Dictionary of Music and Musicians,* as well as *The New Grove Dictionary of American Music,* are invaluable resources. Also of interest is H. Wiley Hitchcock's *Music in the United States: An Historical Introduction.* Carol Oja's fascinating *Making Music Modern,* a look at musical New York in the 1920s, the era of Copland's *Piano Variations* and Ives's retreat, is not only an excellent read, but also a thorough examination of that complex period. She makes it come to life, rather than entombing it in scholarship. Nicholas Slonimsky's *Music Since 1900* is also an excellent general resource, as is Wilfred Mellers's *Music in a New Found Land: Themes and Developments in the History of American Music.*

The reigning thinker on the state of American music in this century is Joseph Horowitz, whose seminal *Understanding Toscanini,* as well as his lesser-known *The Post-Classical Predicament, Dvorak in America,* and *Wagner Nights,* should be required reading for American musicians today, especially composers.

Leonard Bernstein's Charles Eliot Norton Lectures, entitled *The Unanswered Question* in either their book or video form, are fascinating. They not only address the idea of a universal musical grammar (via the theories of Noam Choamsky), but outline the crisis of the recently passed musical century.

# Selected Bibliography

Berger, Arthur. *Aaron Copland*. New York: Oxford University Press, 1953.

Bernstein, Leonard. *The Unanswered Question: Six Talks at Harvard*. Cambridge: Harvard University Press, 1976.

Copland, Aaron. *Copland on Music*. New York: Doubleday, 1960.

——. *Music and Imagination*. Cambridge: Harvard University Press, 1952.

——. *Our New Music*. New York: McGraw-Hill, 1941.

——. *What to Listen for in Music*. New York: New American Library, 1939.

Ives, Charles. "Essays before a Sonata" from *Three Classics in the Aesthetic of Music*. New York: Dover Publications, 1962.

——. *Memos*. New York: W.W. Norton & Co., 1972.

Perlis, Vivian. *Charles Ives Remembered: An Oral History*. New York: Da Capo Press, 1974.

——. *Copland 1900 Through 1942*. New York: St. Martin's Griffin, 1984.

——. *Copland Since 1943*. New York: St. Martin's Griffin, 1989.

Pollock, Howard. *Aaron Copland: The Life and Work of an Uncommon Man*. Urbana: University of Illinois Press, 1999.

Swafford, Jan. *Charles Ives: A Life with Music*. New York: W. W. Norton & Co., 1996.

# CD Track Listing

1. COPLAND: Concerto for Clarinet and String Orchestra, with Harp and Piano (16:44)

   Richard Stoltzman, clarinet; Michael Tilson Thomas, conductor, London Symphony Orchestra

   ℗ 1993 BMG Music. Courtesy of BMG Classics, a unit of BMG Music.

2. COPLAND: *Appalachian Spring* (24:55)

   Eugene Ormandy, conductor, Philadelphia Orchestra

   Originally recorded prior to 1972. All rights reserved by BMG Music. Courtesy of BMG Classics, a unit of BMG Music.

3. COPLAND: *El Salón México* (11:35)

   Eduardo Mata, conductor, Dallas Symphony Orchestra

   ℗ 1978 BMG Music. Courtesy of BMG Classics, a unit of BMG Music.

4. IVES: *The Unanswered Question* (6:12)

   Glenn Fischthal, trumpet; Michael Tilson Thomas, conductor, San Francisco Symphony

   ℗ 2002 BMG Music. Courtesy of BMG Classics, a unit of BMG Music.

5. IVES: "Memories" (2:30)

   Michael Tilson Thomas, piano; Thomas Hampson, baritone

   ℗ 2002 BMG Music. Courtesy of BMG Classics, a unit of BMG Music.
   Thomas Hampson appears courtesy of EMI Classics.

6. IVES: "General William Booth Enters into Heaven" (5:44)

Thomas Hampson, baritone; Michael Tilson Thomas, conductor, San Francisco Symphony and Chorus

Ⓟ2002 BMG Music. Courtesy of BMG Classics, a unit of BMG Music. Thomas Hampson appears courtesy of EMI Classics.

7. IVES: *Three Places in New England:* II. "Putnam's Camp" (5:20)

Michael Tilson Thomas, conductor, San Francisco Symphony and Chorus

Ⓟ2002 BMG Music. Courtesy of BMG Classics, a unit of BMG Music.